MONET
THE WATER-LILY POND

CW01635845

ROSS KING

National Gallery Global, London
Distributed by Yale University Press

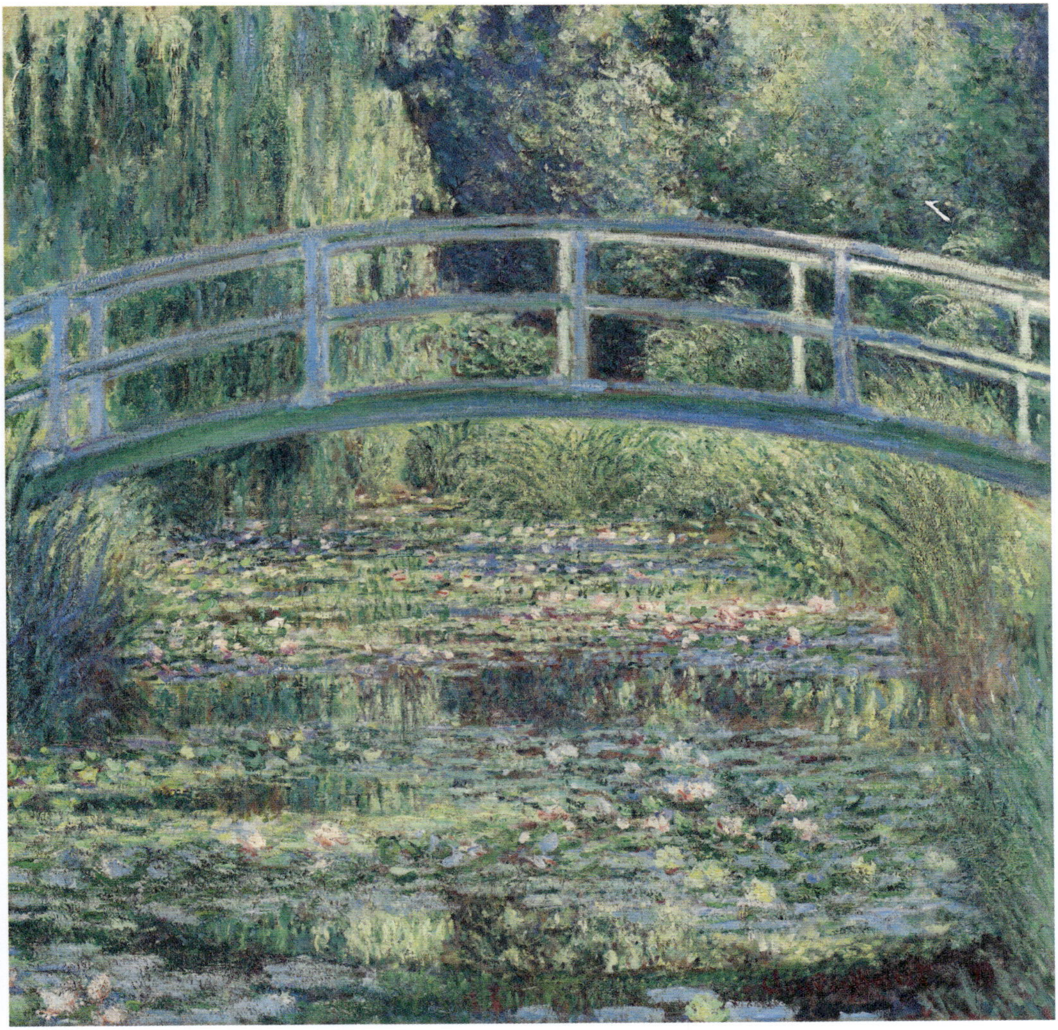

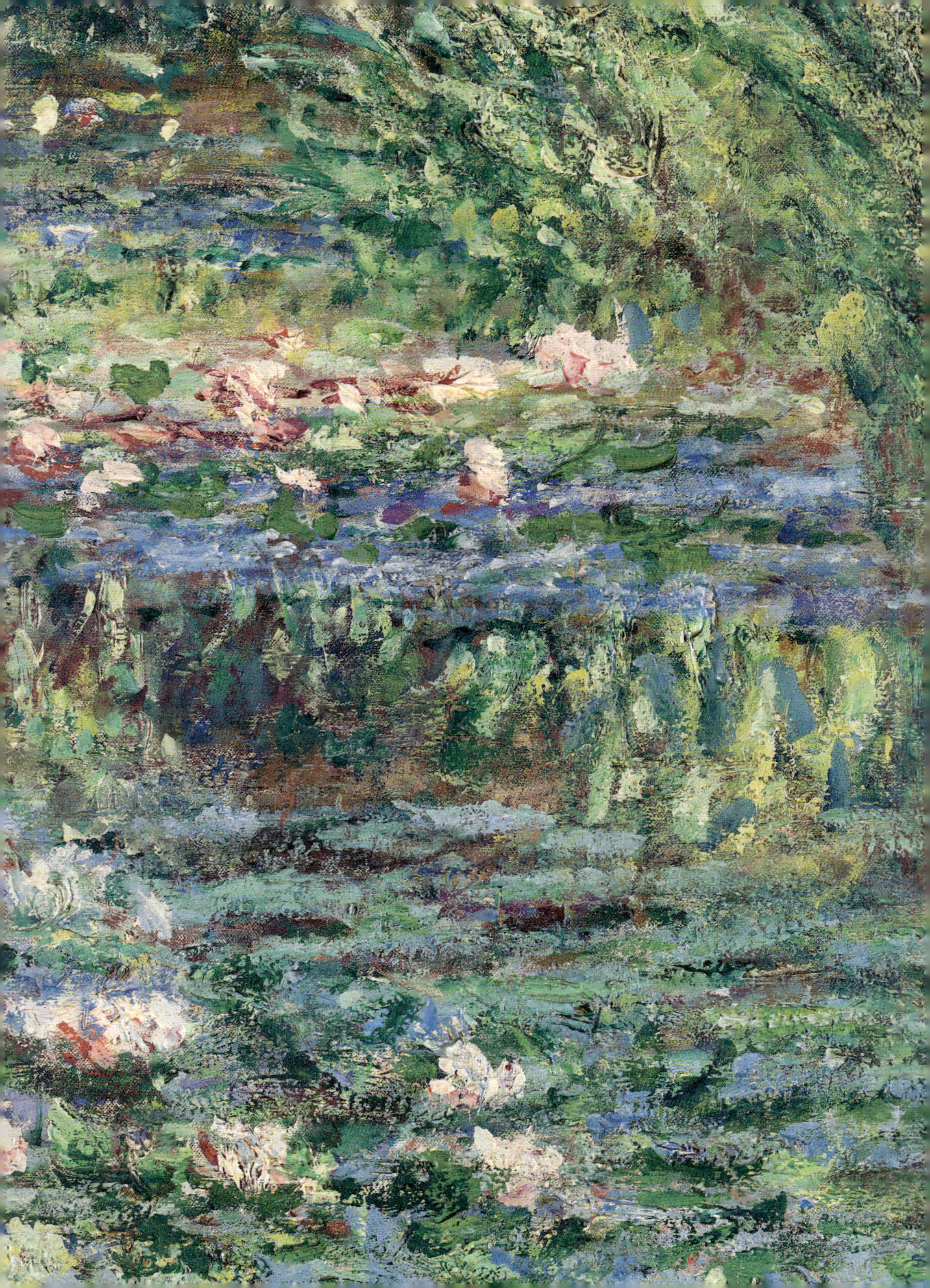

1 *The Water-Lily Pond*, 1899
Oil on canvas, 88.3 × 93.1 cm
The National Gallery, London

A VISIT TO GIVERNY

In the summer of 1897, after chugging along the leisurely meanders of the Seine for a little more than an hour, a locomotive from Paris delivered its passengers to the small town of Vernon, 80 km (50 miles) to the north-west. Disembarking at the station was a 37-year-old journalist and writer from Paris named Maurice Guillemot. Collected by a horse-drawn carriage, he was taken on the three-mile trip to the village of Giverny. Whether by carriage or in one of the new automobiles that had recently begun appearing on France's roads – vehicles running on spoked rubber wheels and powered variously by steam, petrol or electricity – the journey took almost another hour. Guillemot jolted and swayed past cattle grazing in broad meadows and washerwomen at work in the rivulet skirting the road. It was, he wrote, a 'delicious route'.[1]

Giverny itself was home to some 250 people: a cluster of houses, farms and orchards, with a church, two windmills, four taverns and a blacksmith. Halfway through the village, Guillemot found the home of the local celebrity. Claude Monet (1840–1926) had taken possession of this house, pink with green shutters, surrounded by mossy stone walls, in the spring of 1883, at the age of 42 (fig. 2). He had been moving steadily downstream along the Seine from Paris: first to Argenteuil, then to Vétheuil and Poissy, and finally to Giverny, as if returning in stages toward Le Havre, at the mouth of the river on the Normandy coast, where he was raised as a child. These stretches of the Seine and its lush environs had provided many motifs, such as stacks of wheat and fields of poppies, for the canvases that over the past decade had made him one of France's most renowned and successful artists.

Monet had recently begun a new series of landscape paintings showing the Seine in the misty light of dawn (fig. 3). He would rise at 3.30 in the morning and, after his usual cold bath and customary breakfast of marmalade on toast, make his way down to the Seine in hunting boots and a crumpled felt hat. He was always accompanied on the 20-minute walk across the verdant swath of meadow by one of his gardeners (he had eight of them), who transported a dozen or so canvases, each carefully numbered. On the banks of the Seine, the pair would untie the little rowboat moored among the reeds and then, with a few strokes of the oar, reach the flat-bottomed boat that Monet used as his studio. Here, hugging the shoreline and deftly switching

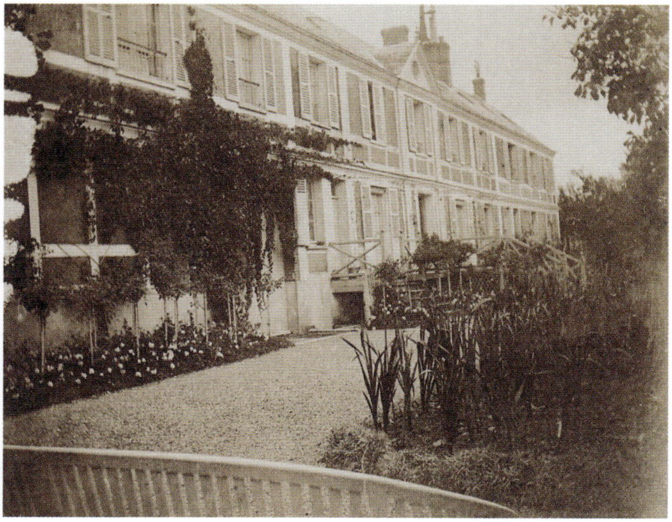

2 Claude Monet's house, Giverny, 1914
Archives of American Art, Smithsonian Institution, Washington DC

3 *Morning on the Seine near Giverny*, 1897
Oil on canvas, 81.6 × 93 cm
The Metropolitan Museum of Art, New York. Bequest of Julia W. Emmons, 1956

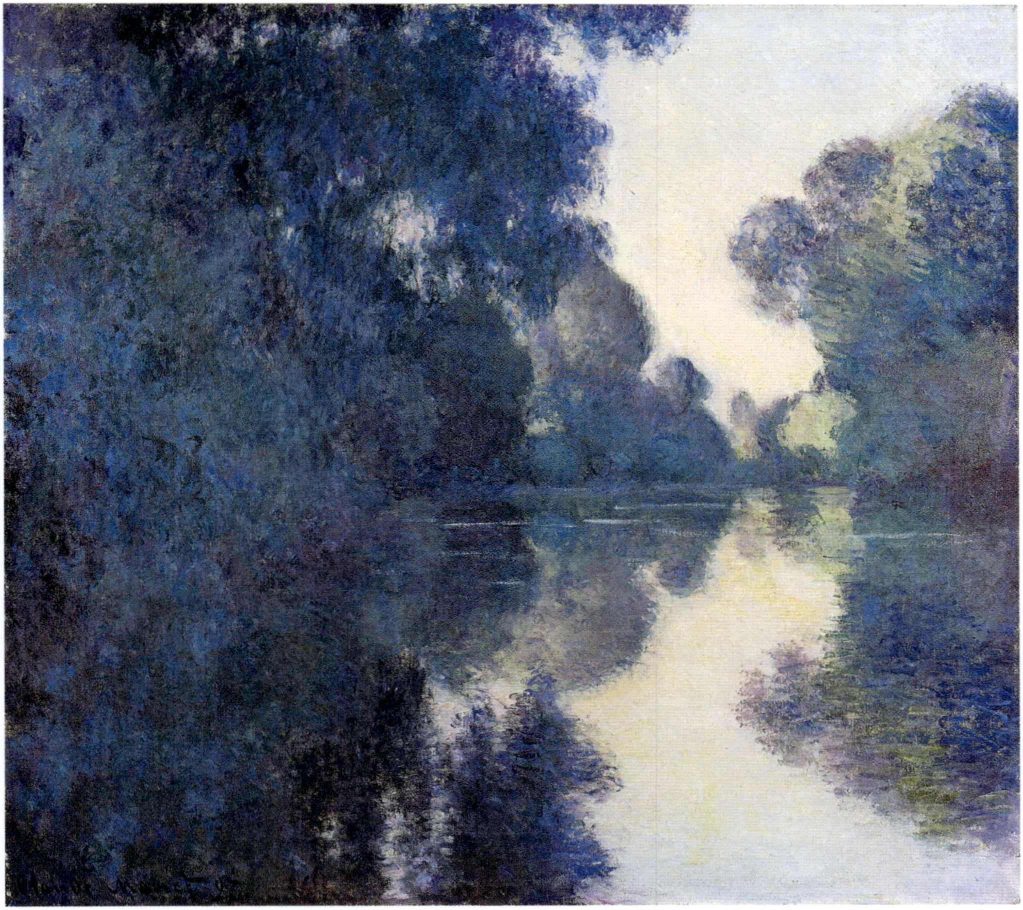

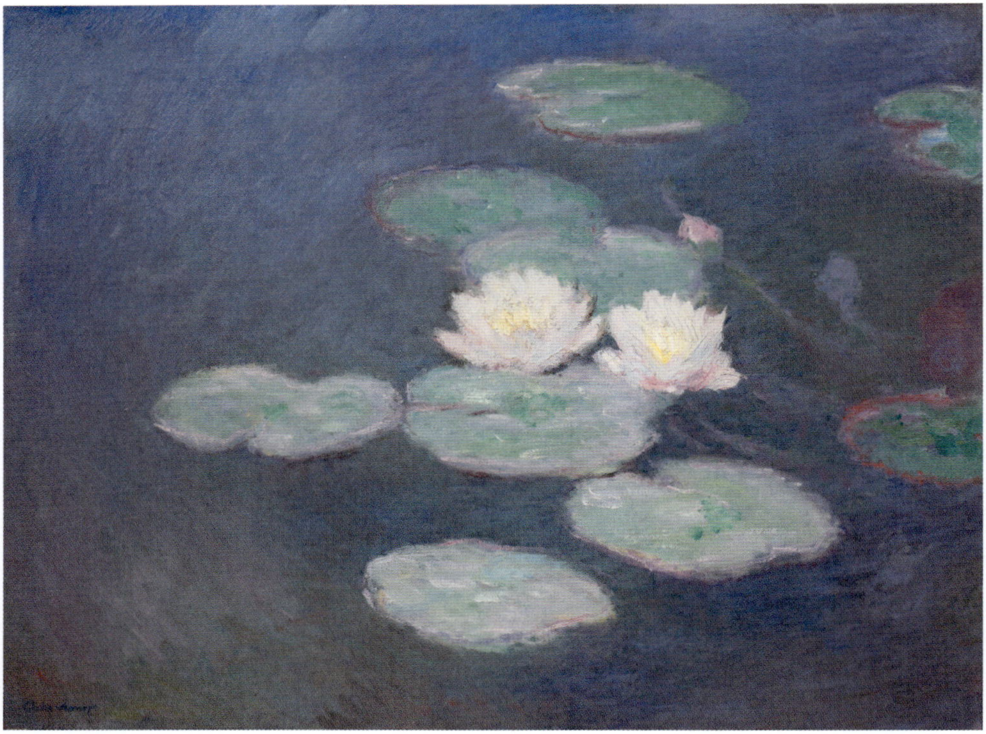

4 *Water Lilies – Evening Effect*, 1897
Oil on canvas, 73 × 100 cm
Musée Marmottan Monet, Paris

from canvas to canvas as the light changed and the hours ticked by, he painted the inlets, the tiny islands and the foliage that loomed overhead and, in the milky dawn light, cast shivering reflections onto the calm but ever-changing surface of the water – pictures of what an enthusiastic critic was soon to call a 'delicious phantasmagoria'.[2]

On the day of his visit in 1897, Guillemot found Monet back at his house following one of these early-morning excursions. After a bell summoned them for lunch, the two men entered a dining room adorned with a ceramic fireplace and a table draped in Russian-embroidered cloth and elegantly arrayed with crystal and fine silverware. The walls, painted a cheery yellow, were hung with dozens of Japanese prints. Lunch was prepared by a cook, Marguerite, whose husband Paul, outfitted in full regalia, served as butler and sommelier. 'You get the best cuisine in France at his house', a later visitor exulted.[3] There was also a housemaid and, toiling away outside, the team of gardeners. A few years later, in 1901, when Monet acquired a Panhard & Levassor, the first of his many automobiles, a chauffeur named Sylvain would join this copious staff.

After lunch, Monet guided his guest down the gravelled garden path, then across a dirt road and a weed-infested railway track before reaching a pond on whose smooth surface floated dozens of water lilies. Sitting under a parasol beside the water, Guillemot was taken by the sight of this strange flora – 'aquatic plants with expansive leaves and disturbingly exotic blooms'. They were to become the motif for Monet's newest landscape paintings, what he called his *paysages d'eau* – 'landscapes of water' (fig. 4). He envisaged these canvases together as an ensemble, decorating a room. He had already begun making a few studies that he showed to Guillemot, who enthusiastically imagined the effect the paintings would have once installed. 'Let us imagine,' he wrote, 'a circular room whose dado would be entirely taken up by a horizon of water spattered with these plants. The walls would seem transparent, alternately green and mauve, with the still and silent water reflecting the spreading flowers. The tones are imprecise, deliciously nuanced, with the delicacy of a dream.'[4]

This description, published by Guillemot in *La Revue illustrée* a few months later, is the first mention we have of the project that would obsess Monet for the last three decades of his long life: the creation of a decorative ensemble of paintings of his artificial pond with its willows and water lilies – what today we would call an installation, offering an immersive experience to spectators. The National Gallery's *The Water-Lily Pond* (see fig. 1), painted in the summer of 1899, two years after Guillemot's visit, serves as one of the precursors to this iconic series, one emblematic of his desire to capture, in a world of his own making, our fleeting visual experiences of nature's cycles and rhythms.

DANGEROUS NOVELTIES

Sturdy and vigorous, with intense eyes and a tanned, weather-beaten face, Oscar-Claude Monet (to give him his full name) looked the part of a gentleman farmer or robust Breton sea captain, or even (as one visitor thought) a 'hunter of wolves and boars' (fig. 5).[5] He was quick of pace and rough of manner, with a gruff voice and a thicket of beard stained yellow from cigarettes. Though he may have looked every inch the provincial rustic, Monet had in fact been born in Paris: 'I am a Parisian from Paris', he once boasted to an interviewer.[6] To be sure, his first home, where he was born in November 1840, had been in rue Laffitte, a street later to become – coincidentally but fittingly – home to numerous art dealers peddling such wares as, by the 1870s, the works of Monet himself. However, Monet's parents left Paris in the mid-1840s and moved to Le Havre, at the mouth of the Seine. With its rugged coast, moody skies and lush meadows, Normandy was to become his spiritual as well as, for most of his life, his actual home.

Le Havre in the 1840s and 1850s was a bustling port city whose strategic location made it a vital hub for international trade, and whose situation on the Normandy coast, which after 1848 could be reached by railway from Paris, turned it into a fashionable resort (fig. 6). Monet's father worked for a well-to-do relative, one of the merchants provisioning the numerous ships that put into the harbour. 'My youth was that of a vagabond', Monet once told an interviewer, but this was sheer romanticism.[7] In fact he enjoyed a comfortable and settled bourgeois upbringing that included Latin and Greek lessons in the local school, concerts in the family home (his mother was a talented singer) and intervals of wandering along the clifftops and bathing in the sea. This comfortable childhood idyll, in a family home 'alive with laughter',[8] was disrupted by his mother's death when he was only 16.

Young Oscar, as he was known in his early years, first found artistic fame around the time his mother died, not with landscapes but as a cartoonist. A bored and reluctant student, he discovered his talent for sketching caricatures when, in the classroom, he began doodling in the margins of his notebooks. 'I represented the faces of my teachers in the most irreverent way,' he recalled, 'deforming them as much as possible.'[9] Hundreds of charcoal drawings followed, showing Le Havre dignitaries peering through monocles or sucking on pipes, with oversize heads, skinny legs and protuberant noses (fig. 7). Caricatures of this sort, or what were known as *portraits charges*, in which facial features were distorted for comic effect, had been enjoying a boom in France.

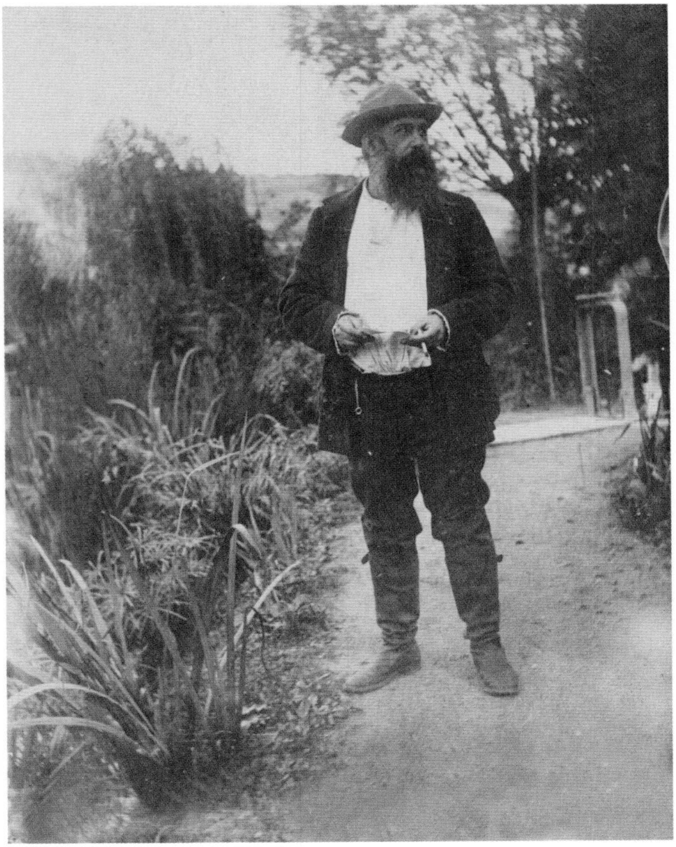

5 Lilla Cabot Perry (1848–1933)
Claude Monet at Giverny, about 1895
Lilla Cabot Perry Photographs, Archives of American Art, Smithsonian Institution, Washington DC

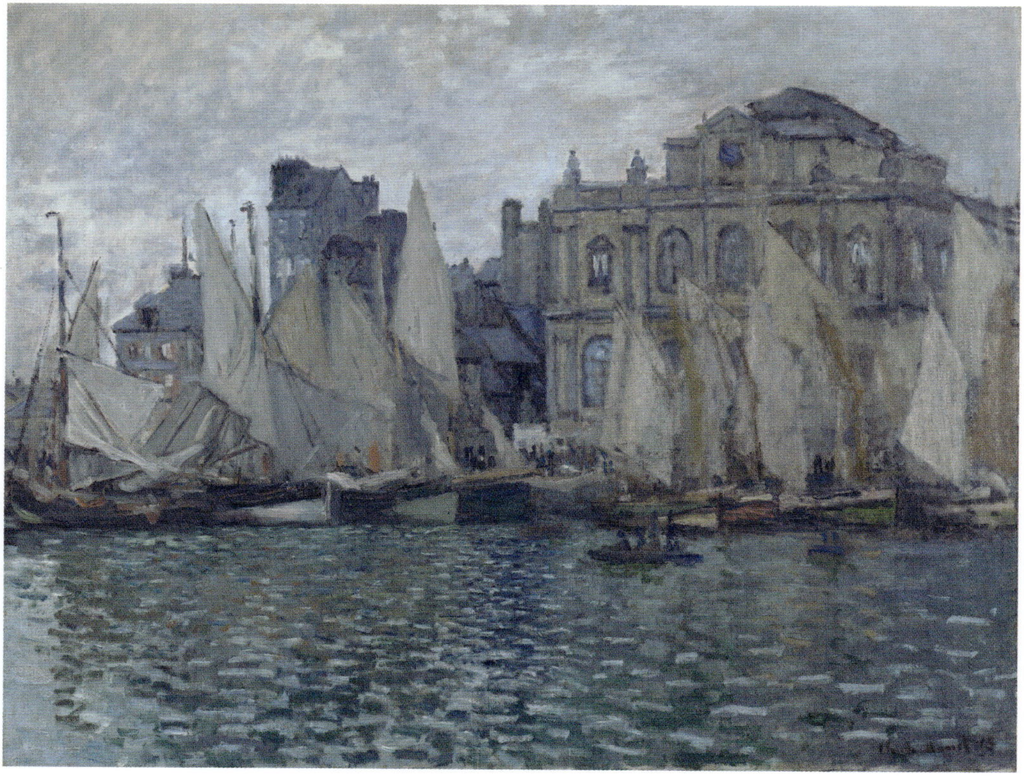

Artists such as Nadar and Etienne Carjat illustrated popular periodicals with *portraits charges* that lampooned famous politicians, actors, singers and composers. The rebellious young Oscar (who made copies of their work to hone his skills) must have appreciated their balloon-pricking mockery as much as he did their nimble draughtsmanship.

The painter who later became the star of so many blockbuster exhibitions first had his work shown in the window of the Gravier Papetier, a framing and stationery shop in Le Havre. Each Sunday evening the proprietor placed Monet's latest caricatures in the window, eliciting much mirth among passers-by (and pride from the artist,

6 *The Museum at Le Havre*, 1873
Oil on canvas, 75 × 100 cm
The National Gallery, London

7 Claude Monet after Etienne Carjat (1828–1906)
Caricature of Mario Uchard, about 1858
Graphite on tan wove paper, 32 × 24.5 cm
The Art Institute of Chicago, Mr and Mrs Carter H. Harrison Collection

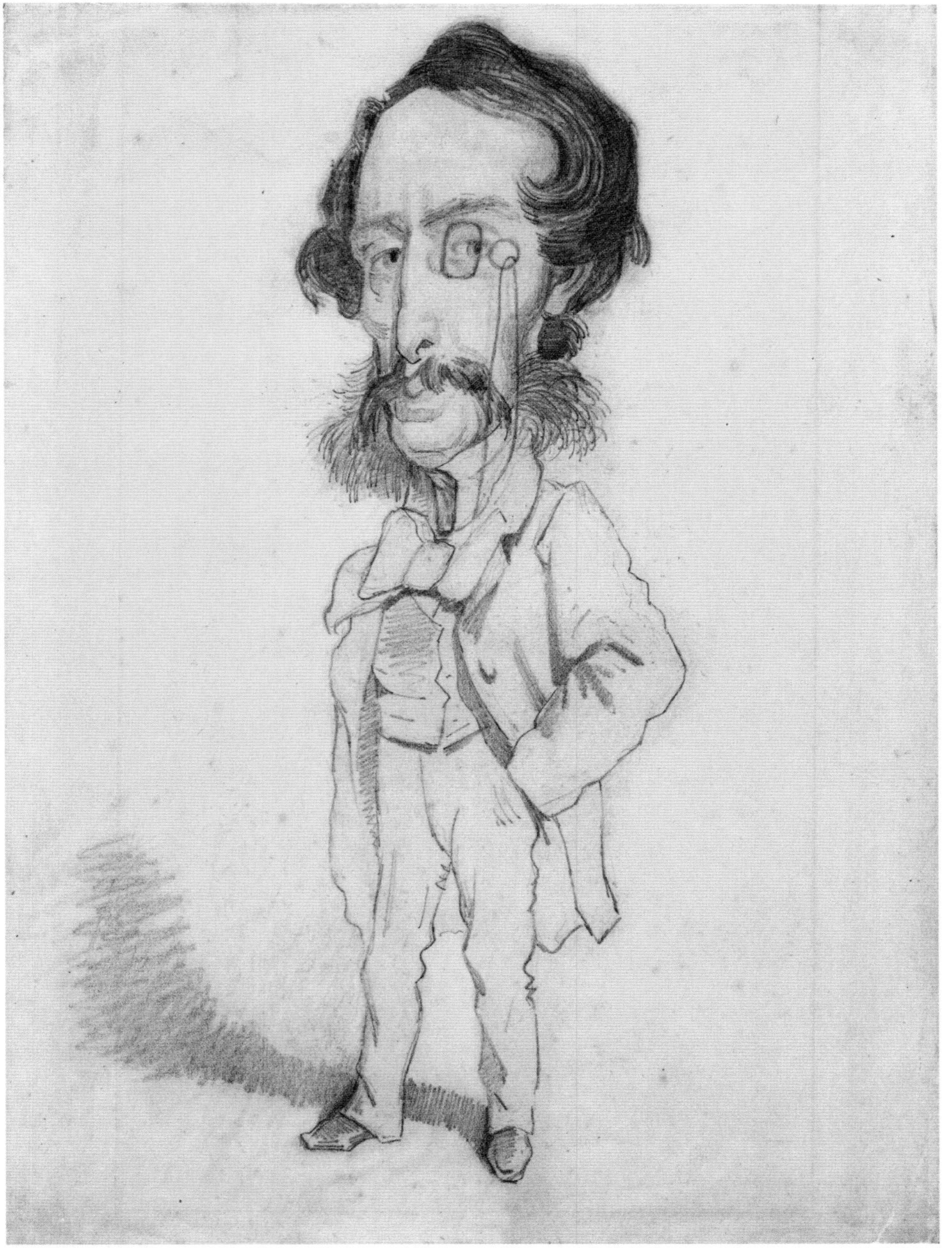

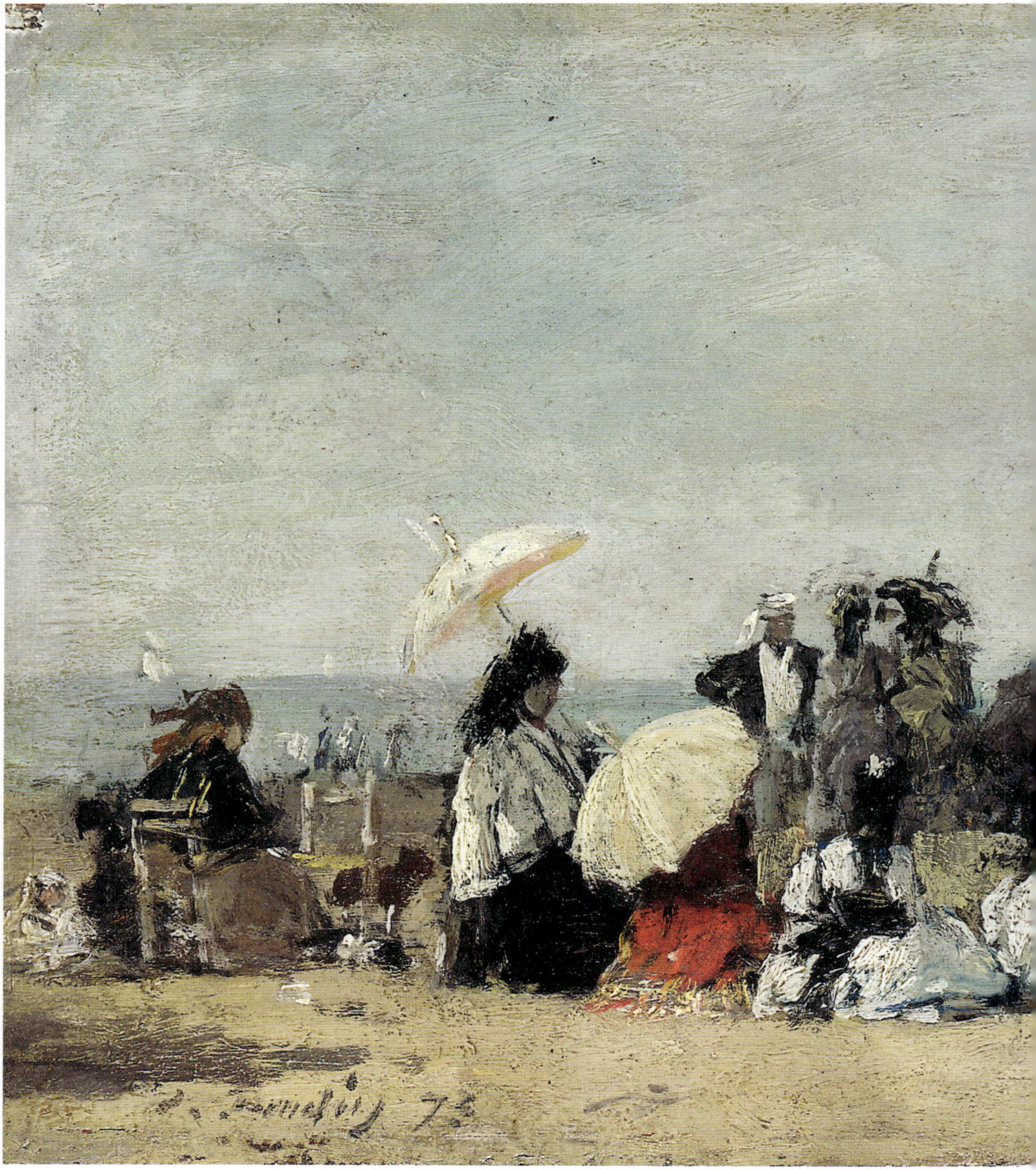

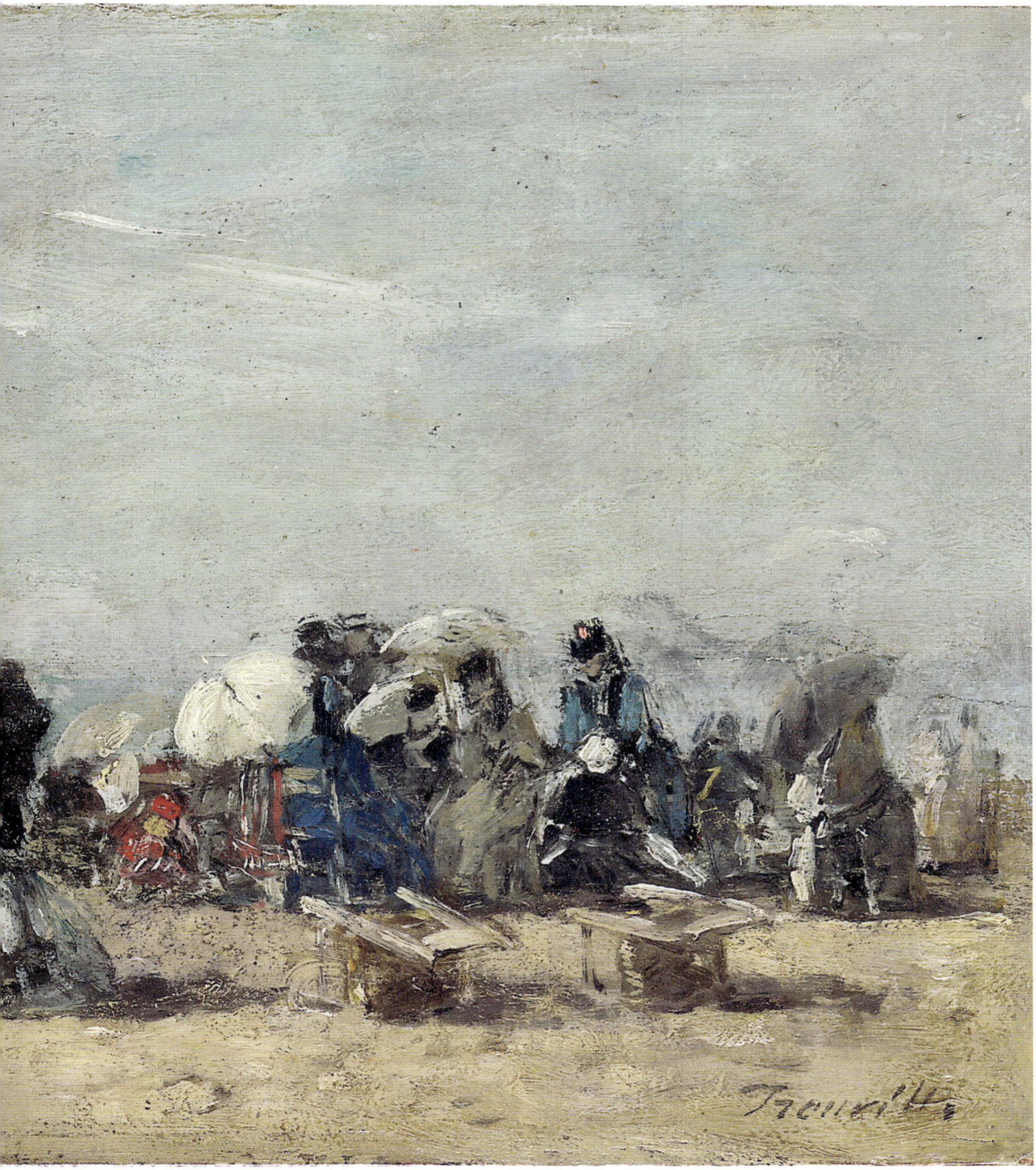

8 Eugène Boudin (1824–1898)
Beach Scene, Trouville, 1873
Oil on wood, 15.5 × 29.9 cm
The National Gallery, London

who lingered within earshot). However, a local artist who shared window space with Monet was less favourably impressed. Eugène Boudin, then in his mid-thirties, had gone to sea at age 14 to work as a cabin boy on ships plying the Channel – something that gave him intimate experience of the region's waters, skies and beaches, which became his chosen subjects. On leaving shipboard life, he had studied painting in Paris thanks to a scholarship from Le Havre's municipal council, and soon earned a reputation, because of his brooding horizons and dramatic clouds, as the 'King of the Skies'. Although Boudin kindly complimented the young artist on the caricatures, he added: 'I hope you won't stop at these.'[10] Boudin later took him on a painting expedition along the coast outside Le Havre – a transformative experience for Monet, who watched mesmerised as Boudin set up his easel on a plateau with a view of the sea, deftly capturing the cliffs and beaches with his brush – subjects to which Monet would later devote himself (figs 8 and 9).

Further lessons with Boudin were to follow before, in 1859, Monet went to Paris to continue his artistic education, which included stints in the vibrant and convivial atmosphere of the Brasserie des Martyrs, a famous hang-out for artists and writers. These pursuits were interrupted in 1861 when, like all young Frenchmen unable to afford to buy themselves out, he was conscripted into the French army. He joined a cavalry regiment, the Chasseurs d'Afrique, not because he liked horses (he never learned to ride) but because he was attracted to the uniform: baggy red trousers, a blue tunic with gold epaulettes and braids, and a red cap known as a kepi (fig. 10). He also claimed to have been enticed by the prospect of derring-do in exotic lands, entertaining visions of 'endless rides in the bright sun, the raids, the crackle of gunpowder, the blows of the sabre, nights under canvas in the desert'.[11]

Monet was duly shipped off to Algeria, then under French colonial rule and subject to widespread resistance movements. He spent a year in North Africa, bewitched by

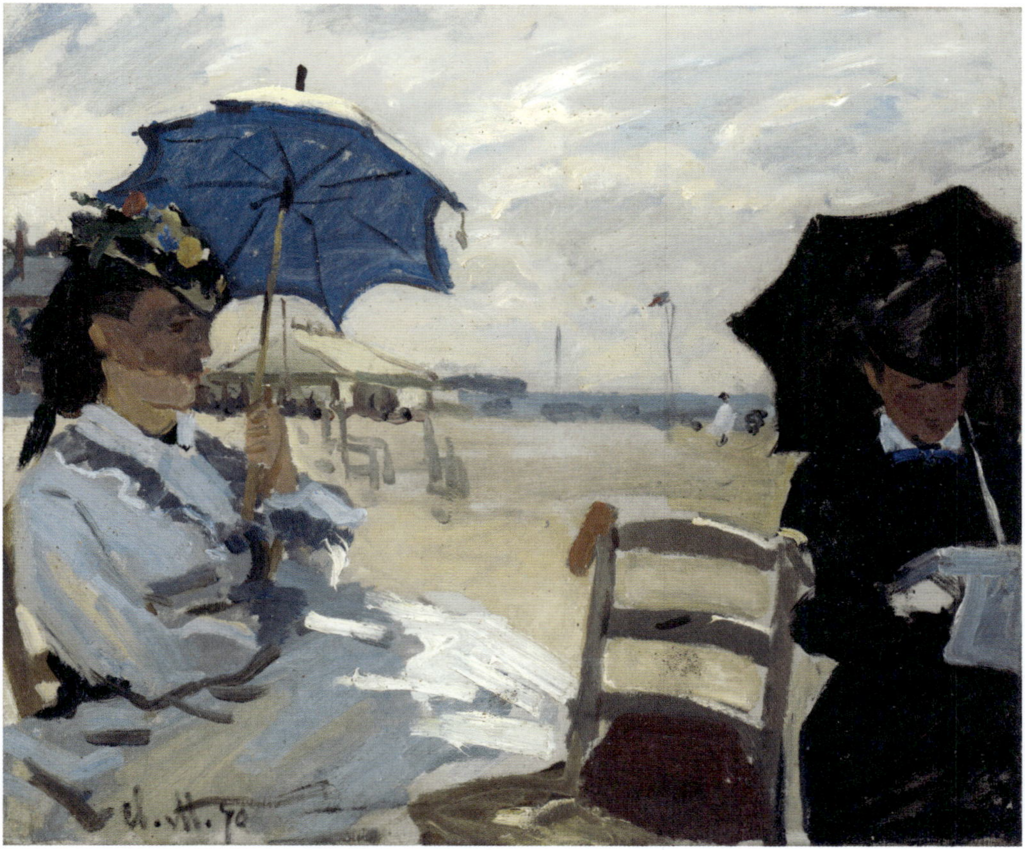

9 *The Beach at Trouville*, 1870
Oil on canvas, 38 × 46.5 cm
The National Gallery, London

the dazzling sunlight, shimmering waters and exuberant flora, though no paintings (if he did any) have survived. He seems not to have performed any sabre-wielding acts of valour, either. Much of his time was spent mucking out stables, before his military career was clouded by an inglorious escapade that witnessed him, ill disciplined as ever, absconding from his barracks on a pack-mule that he crashed into an olive grove. He ended up in the barracks prison followed by – after typhoid fever was diagnosed – the hospital.

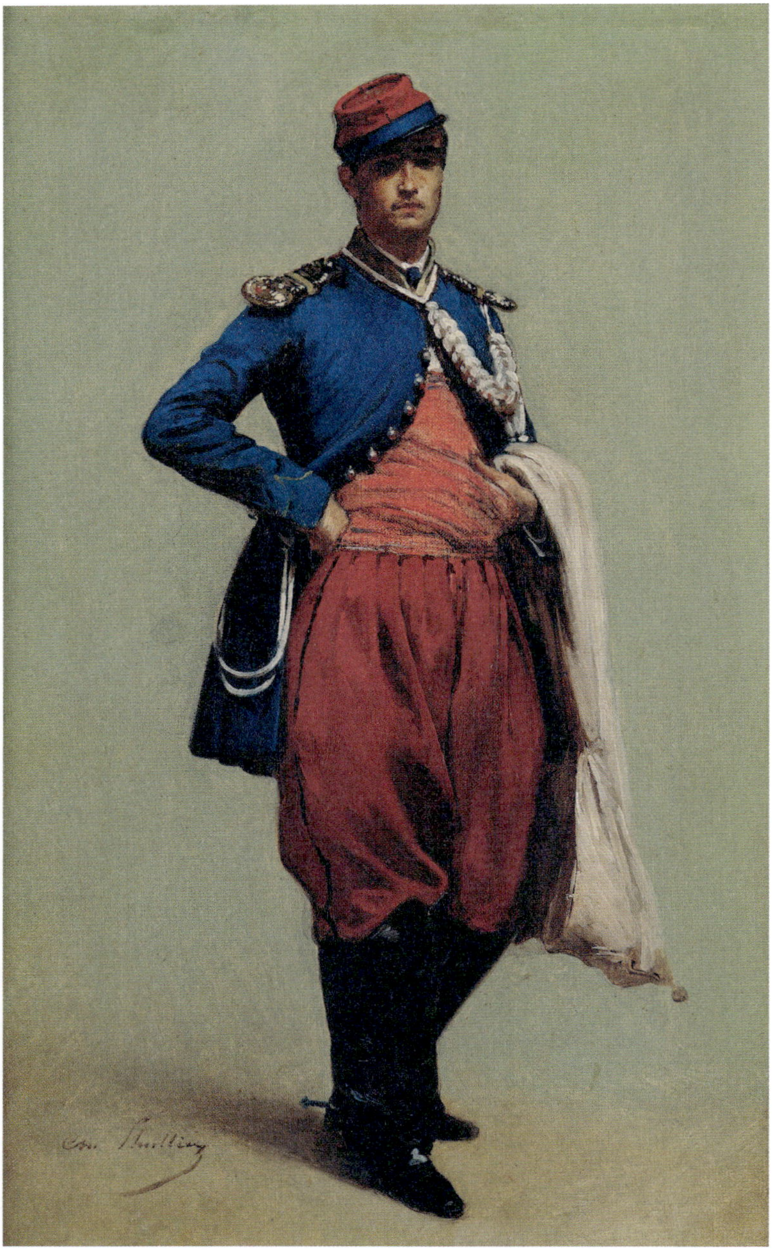

10 Charles Marie Lhuillier (1824–1898)
Portrait of Claude Monet in Uniform, 1861
Oil on canvas, 37 × 24 cm
Musée Marmottan Monet, Paris

Monet resumed his artistic studies after a wealthy aunt bought his way out of the army, despite her reservations and anxieties about his stubborn temperament and wayward behaviour. Back in Paris he fell into the company of other young would-be artists such as Pierre-Auguste Renoir, Frédéric Bazille, Camille Pissarro and Alfred Sisley. He also met his near namesake (with whom he was sometimes confused), Edouard Manet, a painter whose suave and dandyish appearance – frock coat, monocle, cane, yellow gloves, garish trousers – belied a mutinous temperament to match Monet's. What followed was a decade in which this group of rebellious young painters was treated to scorn from the critics, outrage from the public and apathy from the collectors. Their style marked a departure from the 'official' art of France as taught at the Ecole des Beaux-Arts, which emphasised precise draughtsmanship and meticulous brushwork. Students were taught to render every detail, from the folds of fabric to the texture of skin, to create a convincing illusion of reality. Scenes on mythological, historical or biblical themes were encouraged, and above all those that were edifying and heroic. The set topics for the Ecole's annual prize, the Prix de Rome (which entitled the winner to spend five years in Rome, absorbing the artistic styles of Michelangelo and Raphael), included such weighty scenes as *Coriolanus takes Refuge with Tullus, King of the Volscians* (1859) and *Sophocles accused by his Sons* (1860). These episodes were not only dramatic but also intellectually elevated, capable of conveying important moral and political messages. Landscape painting, on the other hand, was seen as a mere imitation of nature without deeper meaning.

Monet and his friends rejected these rigid standards in favour of a more direct and spontaneous approach. They frequently worked (as Boudin had taught Monet to do) outdoors, which allowed them to observe and respond to the natural world around them. Rather than meticulously planning their compositions, they sought to capture light and atmosphere through loose, expressive brushwork and vibrant colour. They also turned from historical and mythological scenes – the endless procession of brandished swords and heaving bosoms – to more contemporary settings. Grand narratives and allegorical themes were replaced by images of modern life, such as operas, ballets, vibrant city streets and leisurely picnics by the river (fig. 11).

The wages of these innovations were, for the most part, critical and commercial death. During the 1860s many of these young painters struggled to get their work shown at the Paris Salon, the annual juried art exhibition. Getting work accepted for the Salon was essential for artists, since it offered the chance for prizes and medals as well as exposure to critics, patrons and the public. However, the jury, composed of established artists of a conservative bent, favoured traditional styles, often rejecting innovative works, which were returned to the artists stamped on the back with an inglorious red 'R' (for *refusé* – refused).

Monet enjoyed some precocious success at the Salons of 1865 and 1866, receiving, as he later boasted, 'unanimous praise'. But his fortunes changed radically over the next few years, when he was 'ignominiously blackballed' for his 'dangerous novelties'.[12] These innovations included experiments using separate, distinct brushstrokes or patches of pure colour to dissolve form and create the illusion of light and space (fig. 12). 'I obtained as much success as I could desire,' he reminisced to Guillemot of those early years; 'that is to say, I was energetically booed by all the critics of the day.'[13]

Unable to sell his work, dunned by creditors, and with a wife (Camille) and young son (Jean) to support, Monet suffered through many difficult years. 'For the past eight days,' he complained to a friend in 1869, 'I've had no bread, no wine, no fire for the kitchen, no light.'[14] He once spent an entire winter living on potatoes. One of his few consolations was the company of Manet and other painters – all likewise struggling – in the Café Guerbois in the Batignolles district of north-west Paris (fig. 13). They became known in the press as the 'Batignolles School', but gained a new name following

11 Pierre-Auguste Renoir (1841–1919)
At the Theatre (La Première Sortie), 1876–7
Oil on canvas, 65 × 49.5 cm
The National Gallery, London

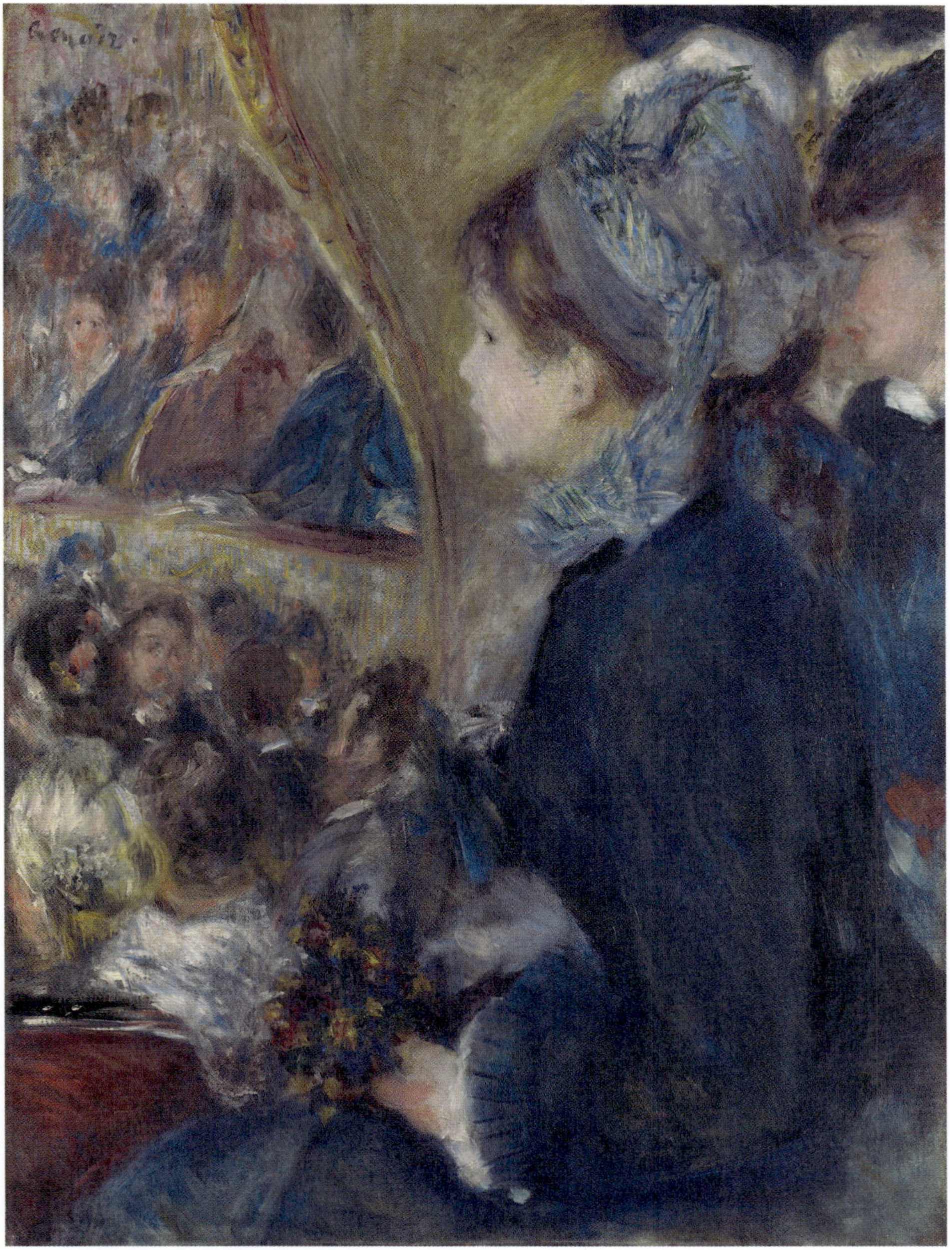
Renoir.

12 *Bathers at La Grenouillère*, 1869
Oil on canvas, 73 × 92 cm
The National Gallery, London

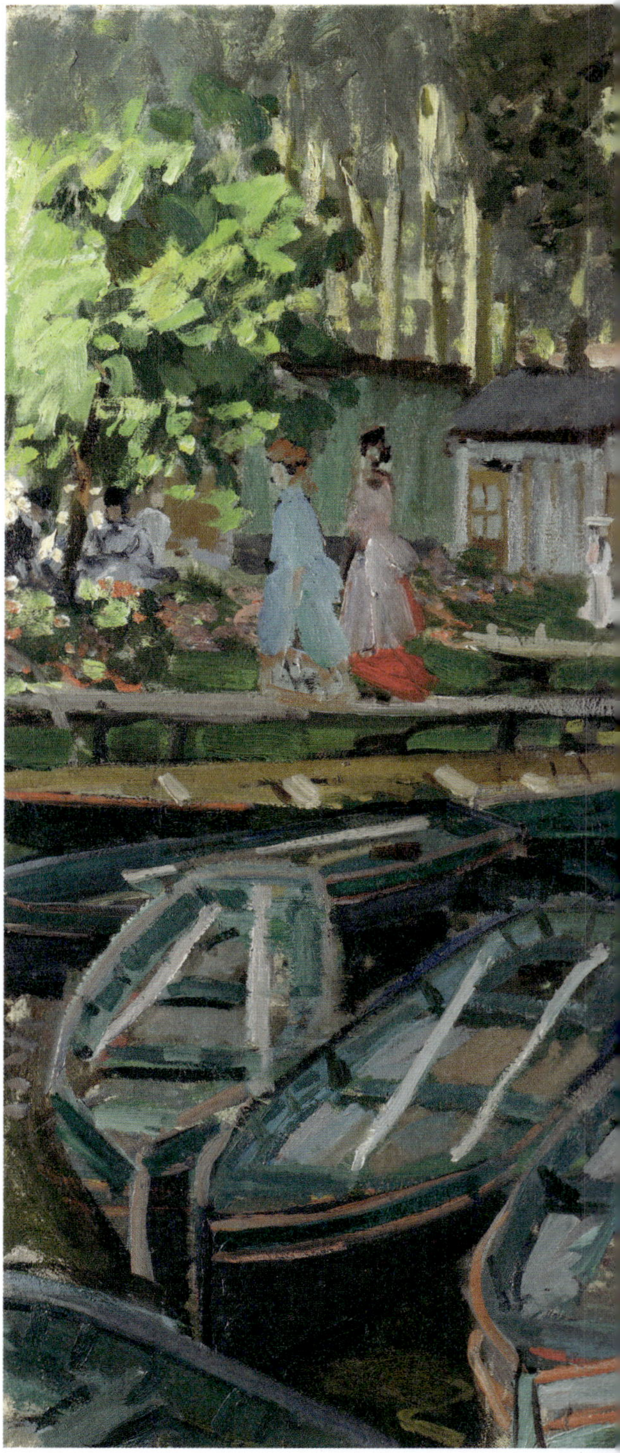

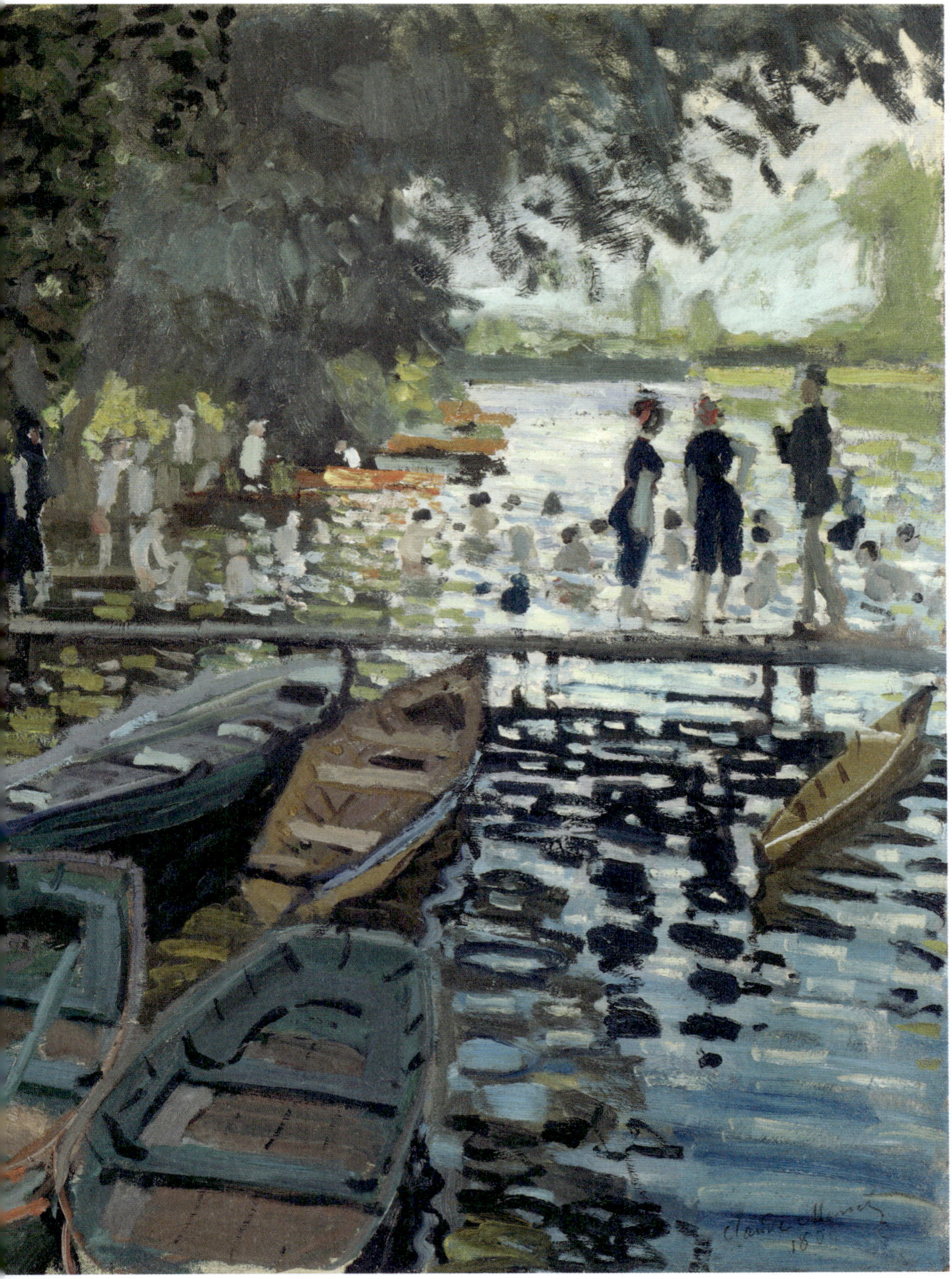

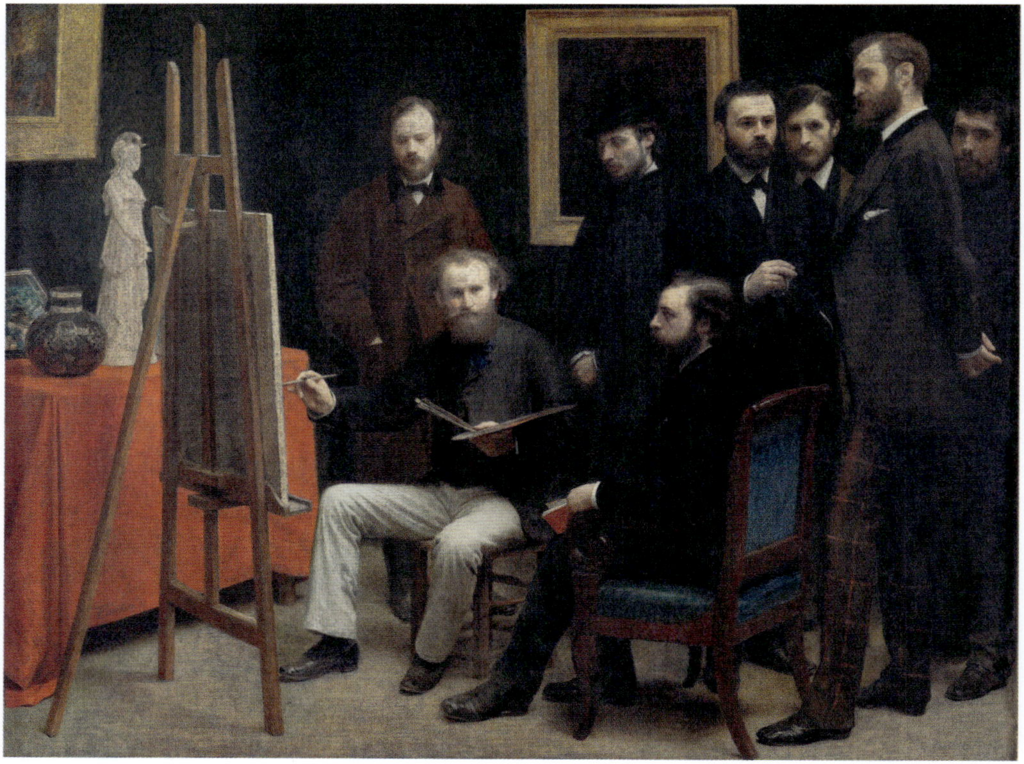

an independent exhibition they staged in Paris in April 1874, following repeated rejection from the official Salon because of their innovative approaches. A critical review of their work by Louis Leroy in *Le Charivari* called them 'impressionists', intended as a derogatory label to describe their sketchy and unfinished style. Leroy had been inspired to use the term by one of Monet's paintings in the exhibition, a view of Le Havre simply entitled *Impression, Sunrise* – a hazy harbour scene in which he used loose brushwork and a delicate palette of oranges and blues to capture the radiant orb of the sun emerging from an ethereal dawn mist (fig. 14). 'Wallpaper in its embryonic state is more finished than that seascape', sniffed Leroy.[15] The painters soon embraced the

13 Henri Fantin-Latour (1836–1904)
A Studio at Les Batignolles, 1870
Oil on canvas, 204 × 273.5 cm
Musée d'Orsay, Paris

name 'Impressionist', recognising that it aptly described their artistic aims and practices.

Seven more Impressionist exhibitions followed in Paris before the last one closed in June 1886. That same year, Monet's Parisian dealer, Paul Durand-Ruel, had the foresight to cross the Atlantic to show the group's work in New York City. Monet was copiously represented, and 36 of his 40 canvases were sold on the strength of enthusiastic reviews proclaiming him 'the most versatile and in many respects the most brilliant painter of the school'.[16] By the late 1880s his long years of struggle had finally ended. Such was his popularity and acclaim in America that by the mid-1890s a woman was overheard remarking: 'Monet is so great that all painters ought to paint Monets.'[17] Her wish appeared to be coming true in certain artistic circles, since by the 1890s many young American painters were attempting to capture the fugitive effects of light and shade with a flickering brushwork they called the 'Giverny trick'.[18] A French art critic came up with a similar name for the Monet-influenced style of young Americans: *givernisme*.[19]

Monet proved as popular with American collectors as he did with American painters. By the 1890s his paintings adorned the homes of senators, stockbrokers and captains of industry. Among the most prolific collectors were Louisine Havemeyer and her husband Harry, the 'sugar king' who at one point controlled 98 per cent of the sugar sold in the United States. The couple would ultimately buy 30 Monet paintings for their turreted, Tiffany-decorated mansion on Fifth Avenue in New York. Monet was even more abundantly represented in the neo-Gothic mansion in Chicago of Bertha Honoré Palmer. The wife of a dry goods tycoon, Palmer purchased 90 Monet paintings (more than 20 in a single shopping spree in 1891) to go with her collection of Tang vases and Louis XVI furniture.

Monet was enjoying popularity and esteem in France as well, largely due to his series of paintings intensely focused on the French landscape. He had become fascinated with the

14 *Impression, Sunrise*, 1872
Oil on canvas, 75 × 91 cm
Musée Marmottan Monet, Paris

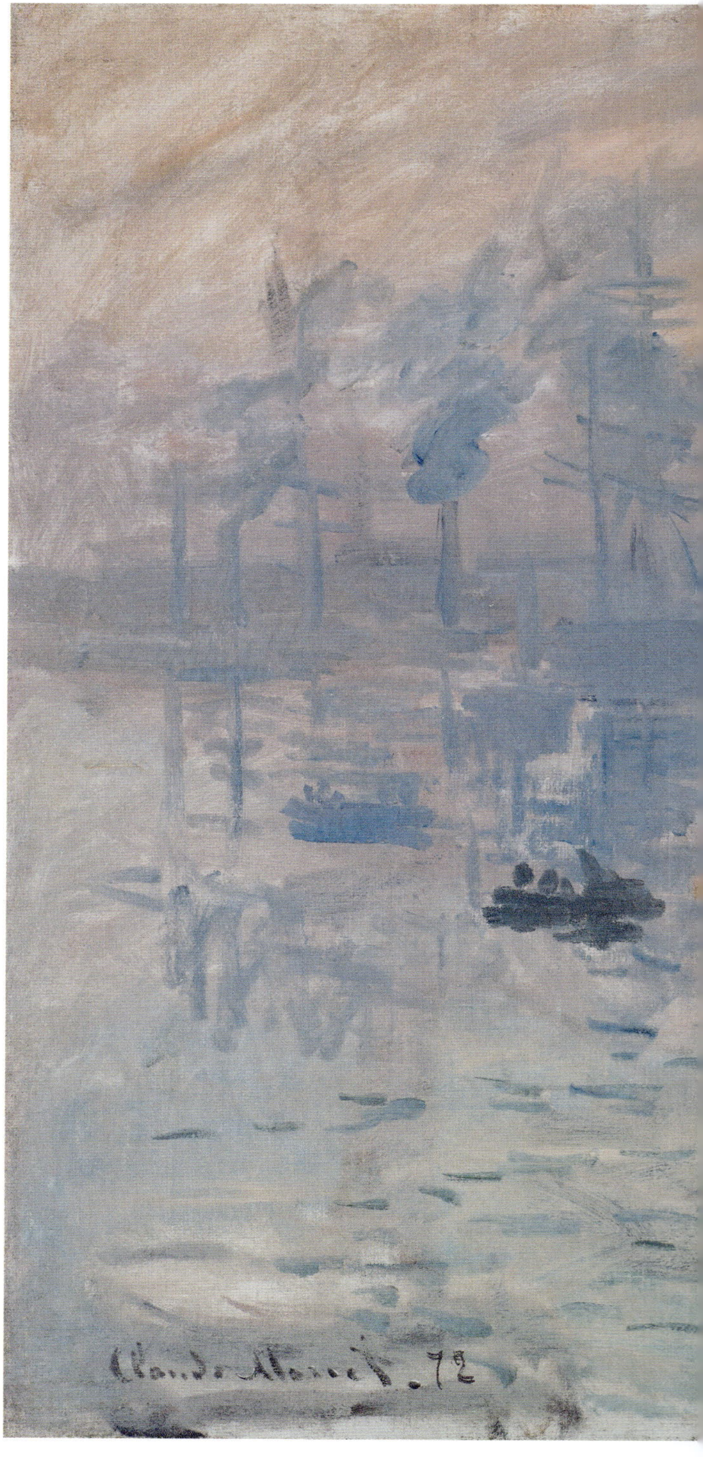

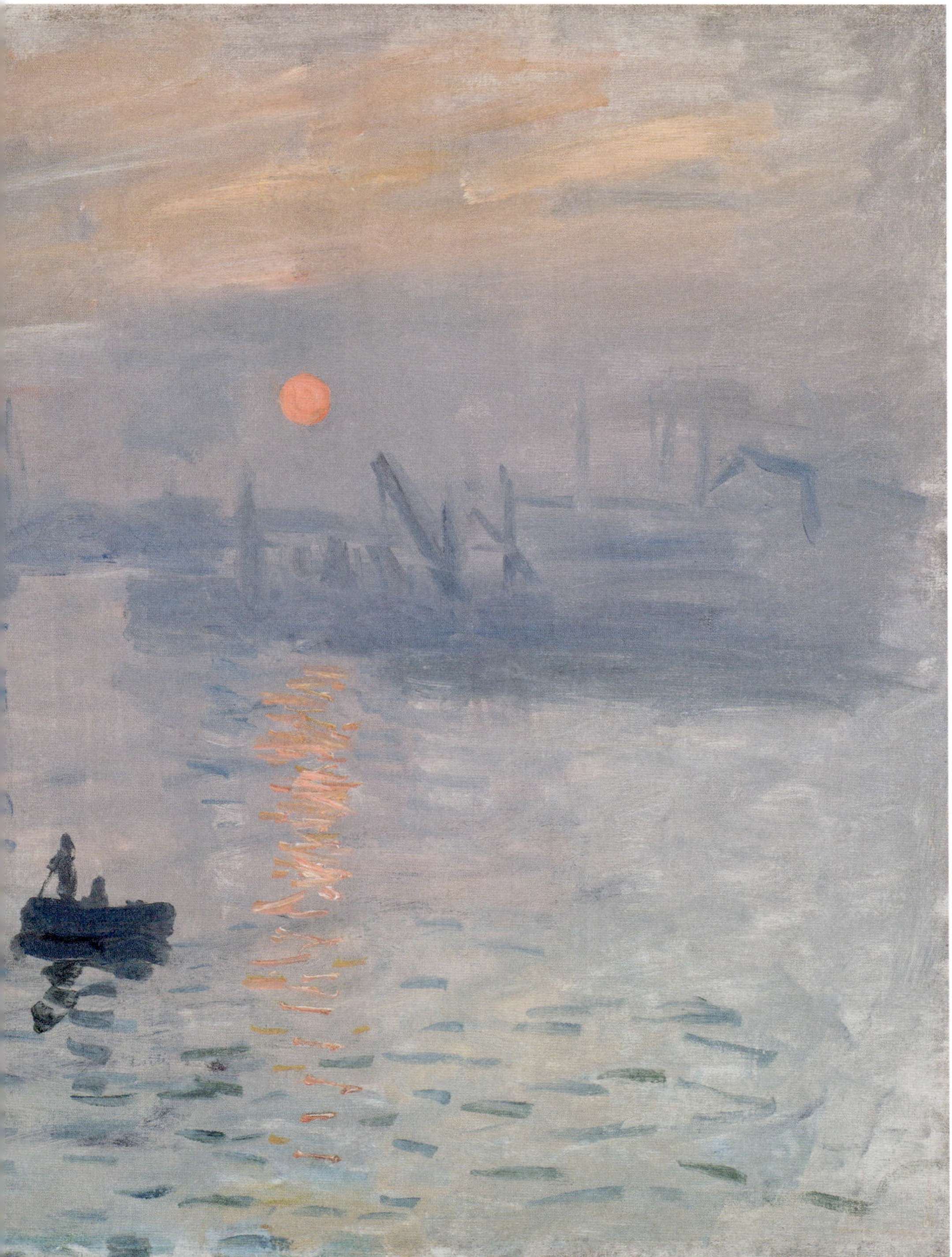

idea of capturing the same subject under different lighting conditions and at various times of the day or year. If previously he had moved his easel and canvases around fields and riverbanks in search of particular views, now he hunkered down in front of a chosen subject for weeks or even months on end, obsessively painting one canvas after another. In the summer of 1890, turning his attention to the grainstacks in the meadow outside Giverny, he began producing multiple paintings of the same subject, forming a cohesive series – more than 25 canvases – that explored the nuances of colour, light and atmosphere (figs 15 and 16). These paintings, exhibited at the Galerie Durand-Ruel in May 1891, were followed by a series of poplars lining the lazy swerve of the Epte river, exhibited at Durand-Ruel in 1892. He then produced more than 30 paintings of the facade of Rouen cathedral, staring at the massive monument with such sustained intensity – 10 hours a day for weeks on end – that he suffered nightmares of the building toppling onto him (fig. 17).

The reason for these obsessive painting sessions was Monet's pursuit of the transitory appearances of the natural world – his attempt to capture and immortalise on canvas a succession of ever-changing moments. He concentrated on how the appearances of objects were constantly transformed with the seasons, the weather, the time of day and the light (which he believed changed every seven minutes). One admiring critic called these canvases a record of 'a series of infinite transitions in which each new day reconstitutes, under the changing light, an object which never was and never will be again'.[20] More than the objects themselves, it was the atmosphere surrounding them that fascinated him, the ethereal dance of light and colour that he called the *enveloppe*.

During his visit in 1897, Guillemot was not only witness to Monet's work on the gauzy *enveloppe* shrouding the Seine at daybreak – the series that became known as *Mornings on the Seine*. He also saw Monet's first attempts at what was to become his newest and most lasting obsession, and the repository of his greatest artistic aspirations: his water-lily pond.

15 *Grainstacks: Snow Effect*, 1891
Oil on canvas, 65 × 92 cm
National Galleries of Scotland, Edinburgh

16 *Stacks of Wheat (Sunset, Snow Effect)*, 1890–1
Oil on canvas, 65.3 × 100.4 cm
The Art Institute of Chicago, Potter Palmer Collection

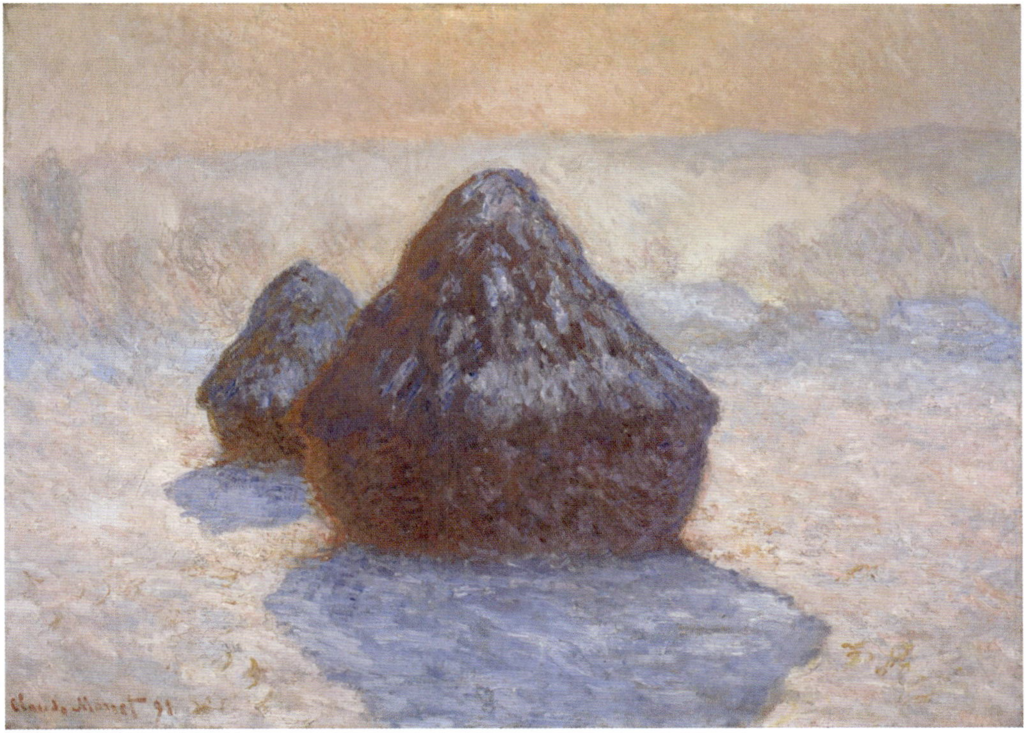
Claude Monet 91

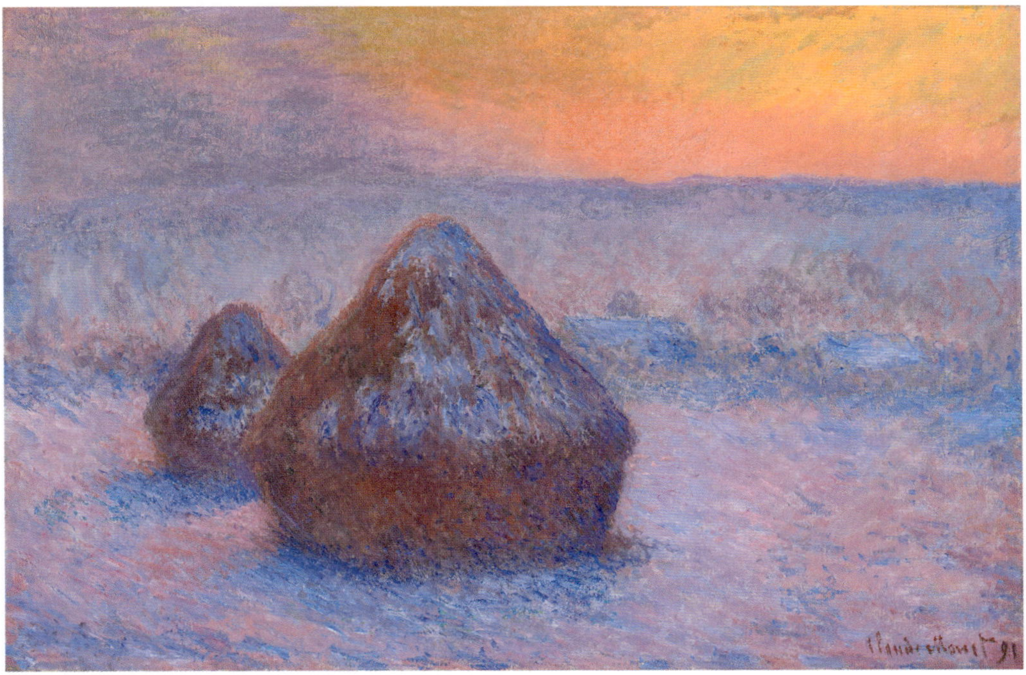
Claude Monet 91

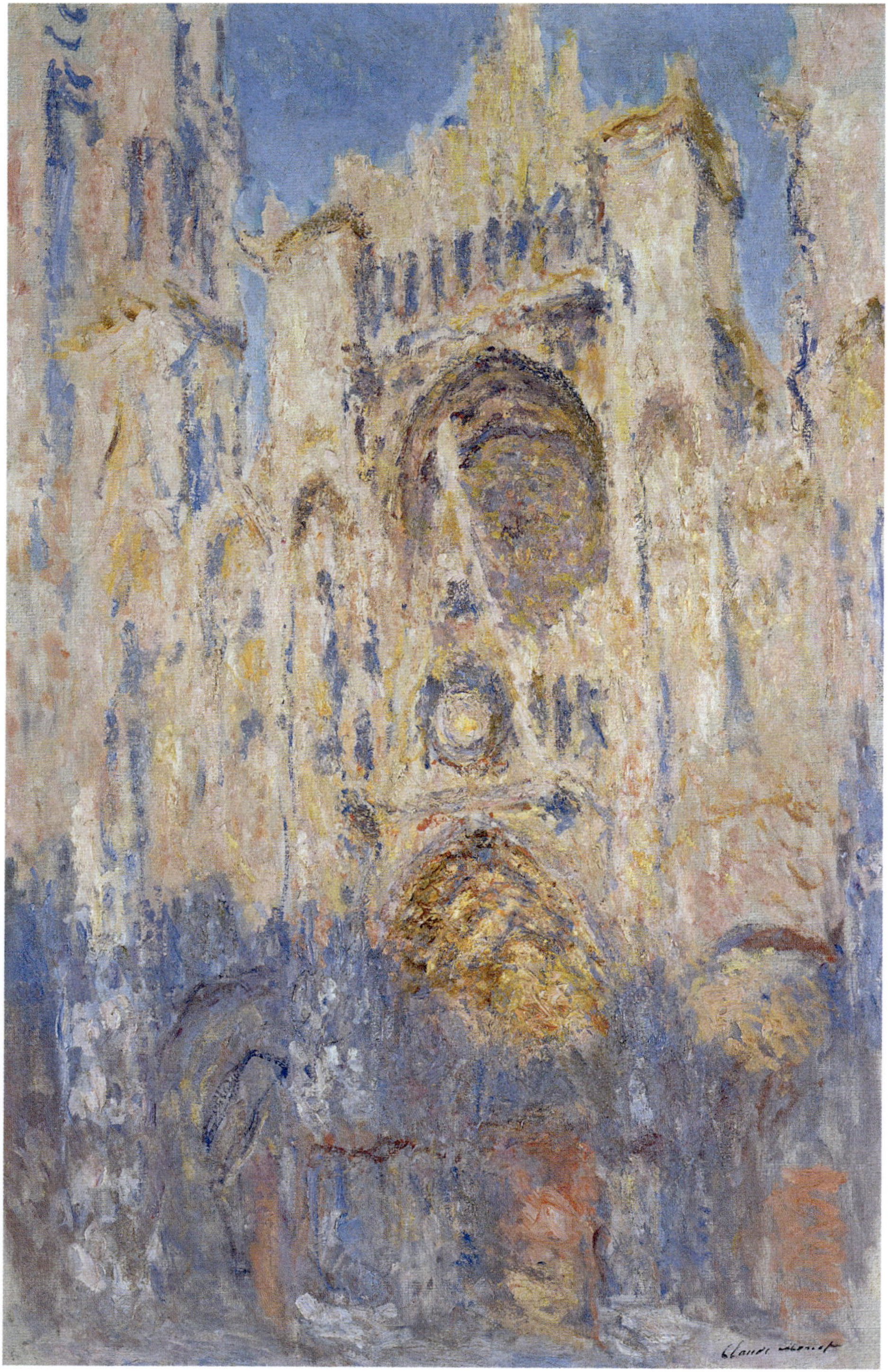

LES JAPONAIS

Monet had begun creating his water-lily pond four years earlier. In 1893 he purchased a strip of marshland beyond the railway tracks at the bottom of his garden, then proceeded to divert a stream, a tributary of the Epte, to feed a pond. A year later he planted the pond with water lilies and other aquatic plants such as bog cotton. Water lilies had been one of the many attractions at the 1889 Exposition Universelle, or World's Fair, in Paris, the international trade exhibition for which the Eiffel Tower – complete with four restaurants, a beer hall and a Viennese bakery serving waffles – was constructed as an entrance arch and ticket kiosk (fig. 18). A horticulturalist named Joseph Bory Latour-Marliac exhibited nine species of water lily in the ponds of the Trocadéro, across the Seine from the Eiffel Tower. Latour-Marliac had abandoned a law career in 1875 to open a nursery in south-west France that catered to the growing taste in French gardens for colour, novelty, variety and exoticism – for stunning blooms and luxuriant foliage. For much of the nineteenth century, botanists and plant hunters had been introducing Europeans to new varieties of flowers from Asia, Africa and South America, as well as creating hybrids and cultivars. Latour-Marliac achieved success when he crossed the hardy European water lily, whose flowers were white, with more colourful tropical species from Mesoamerica. By the late 1880s he was producing water lilies with flowers of pink, lilac, canary yellow and bright red. Put on display in the ponds at the Trocadéro, they were awarded a gold medal, while their 'abundant flowering' (according to an official report) 'was admired by visitors and connoisseurs'.[21]

It is not surprising that Monet should have made his way through the maze of kiosks and pavilions to the horticultural exhibits at the Trocadéro. Such was his obsession with gardens that Guillemot claimed he read horticultural journals and plant catalogues more avidly than periodicals about art. For many decades he had depicted gardens in his paintings, including those of his own design such as his gladioli- and

17 *Rouen Cathedral, Sun Effect, End of the Day*, 1892
Oil on canvas, 100 × 65 cm
Musée Marmottan Monet, Paris

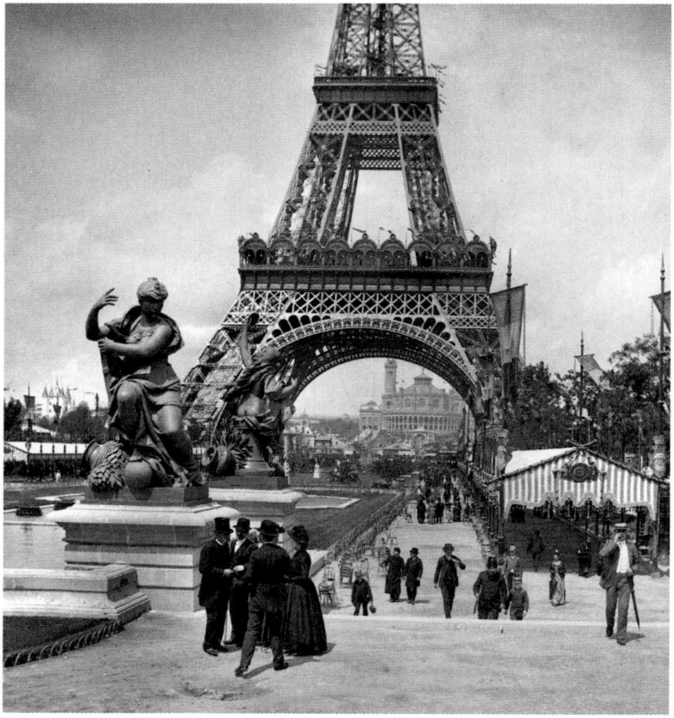

18 The Eiffel Tower and view of the grounds at the Exposition Universelle, 1889

19 Lilla Cabot Perry (1848–1933)
The Japanese bridge on Monet's water-lily pond, about 1895
Lilla Cabot Perry Photographs, Archives of American Art, Smithsonian Institution, Washington DC

dahlia-filled suburban patch at Argenteuil in the mid-1870s. The sight of Latour-Marliac's colourful plants floating on a mirror-like surface of water inspired him to create his own water garden, one meant to 'please the eye', as he wrote to a friend, but also, crucially, to provide 'motifs to paint'.[22] Five years after Monet saw the display at the Trocadéro, his pond was finally ready and he placed an order with Latour-Marliac for more than 70 aquatic plants, including water chestnut, marsh marigold, Egyptian lotuses and six water lilies, yellow and pink in colour. The lotuses quickly perished despite Latour-Marliac's assurances that they were capable of surviving the Normandy winter. The water lilies, on the other hand, thrived. Monet later ordered more, including the *Nymphaea* 'Atropurpurea' with its striking crimson flowers and large, saucer-shaped leaves. The local farmers, whose livestock grazed the nearby meadows and drank from the stream, had been alarmed at the sight of these alien blooms – the ones that Guillemot found 'disturbingly exotic'. They feared for their cattle, claiming that Monet was poisoning the water. But he had been scornfully impervious to their concerns. 'To hell with the Giverny residents', he growled.[23] Not for nothing did he have among the locals, according to Guillemot, 'a reputation for savagery'.

Soon after the water lilies arrived, Monet added something else to his pond: a Japanese-style bridge that spanned the water at its narrowest stretch (fig. 19). It is unclear where or when Monet first encountered Japanese

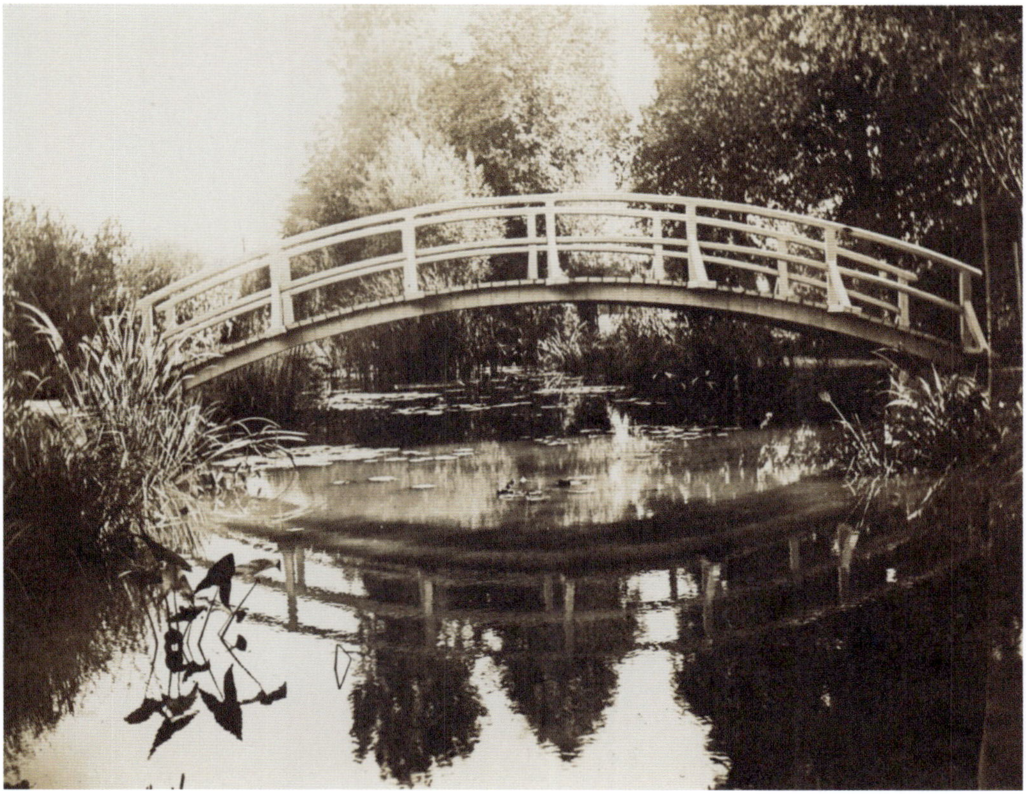

bridges. He could have seen them at the World's Fair in Paris in 1878, when the Japanese pavilion, described enthusiastically in a guidebook as 'one of the main attractions' of the fair, featured a garden with 'pretty arched bridges'.[24] He could have seen them again, more recently, at the 1889 World's Fair. The garden in the Japanese pavilion was designed by Wasuke Hata, whose triumph was such that the next two decades witnessed a craze among wealthy French landowners for Japanese gardens, complete with pagodas, tea rooms and bridges. Hata laid out a series of these gardens in and around Paris for wealthy clients such as Edmond de Rothschild, the Countess de Greffulhe and the photographer Hugues Krafft. Another enthusiast was the banker Albert Kahn, a neighbour of Rothschild's in Boulogne-Billancourt. His garden featured exotic plants sent to him by the Emperor of Japan, along with a red-lacquered bridge – one that replicated the famous Shinkyo Bridge – specially constructed by Japanese carpenters.

Monet's Japanese bridge was built at around the same time as these other gardens were laid out. Footbridges were traditional features of Japanese gardens, and arched or crescent-shaped bridges, known as 'moon bridges', were particularly iconic. These bridges were used for, among other things, moon-viewing ceremonies, in which participants gazed at the beauty of the moon and its changing phases. Positioned over ponds or streams, the bridges provided not only a vantage point for viewing the moon in the sky but also for seeing its reflection in the water. The poetic and symbolic atmosphere was enhanced by the bridge's semicircular shape – like a crescent moon. Additionally, the bridges catered to what an English handbook of the time called 'the love of picturesqueness' and the 'fondness for lingering above an expanse of water, to enjoy the cool breezes and watch the goldfish disporting in the stream'.[25] Monet's bridge likewise became a place from which to gaze at the waters and the water lilies below, while it also, of course, provided a motif for him to paint.

A visitor once claimed that with its bridge, bamboo and peonies, Monet's garden made it seem that 'one was in a suburb of Yokohama'.[26] This distinctly Japanese ambience was probably inspired not so much by actual gardens as by prints and scroll paintings. Monet had supposedly first discovered Japanese art in the Netherlands in 1871, when he encountered a grocer in Zaandam using woodblock prints by Kitagawa Utamaro, Utagawa Hiroshige and Katsushika Hokusai as wrapping paper for coffee and spices. The story about the wrapping paper may have an element of truth since Western trade with Japan had recently opened. Japan had been in self-imposed isolation since 1639, when the Tokugawa shogunate expelled most foreigners to halt Christian conversion efforts, allowing only a few Dutch merchants to remain in a confined area in Nagasaki. However, American interest in Japan grew after renewed trade with China in 1844. On 8 July 1853, Commodore Matthew Perry's US Navy squadron arrived in Edo Bay, demanding the opening of Japanese ports to American ships.

Perry's gunboat diplomacy proved a success. Japan signed the Treaty of Kanagawa with the United States in 1854, soon followed by similar trade deals with France, the Netherlands and England. Japanese commodities then began flooding into the West. But more was to arrive than silk, porcelain, textiles and tea. Because they were relatively inexpensive and widely available in Japan, prints by artists such as Hiroshige and Hokusai were used as packing or wrapping material for fragile exports such as blue and white porcelain. According to various legends, these prints were discovered and cherished by Western artists such as Félix Bracquemond and James McNeill Whistler. The impact of these woodblock prints on Western artists was tremendous. As this artistic New World hove suddenly into view, many of them began imitating the unique perspectives, unusual croppings, intricate stylisations and areas of bright, unshaded colour favoured by Japanese artists. So profound was the influence on the Impressionists

Overleaf:
20 Utagawa Hiroshige (1797–1858)
Sudden Shower over Shin-Ōhashi Bridge and Atake from *One Hundred Famous Views of Edo*, 1857
Woodblock print; ink and colour on paper, 34 × 24.1 cm
The Metropolitan Museum of Art, New York. The Howard Mansfield Collection, Purchase, Rogers Fund, 1936

21 Utagawa Hiroshige (1797–1858)
In the Kameido Tenjin Shrine Compound, from *One Hundred Famous Views of Edo*, 1856
Woodblock print; ink and colour on paper, 36.2 × 24.8 cm
The Metropolitan Museum of Art, New York. The Howard Mansfield Collection, Purchase, Rogers Fund, 1936

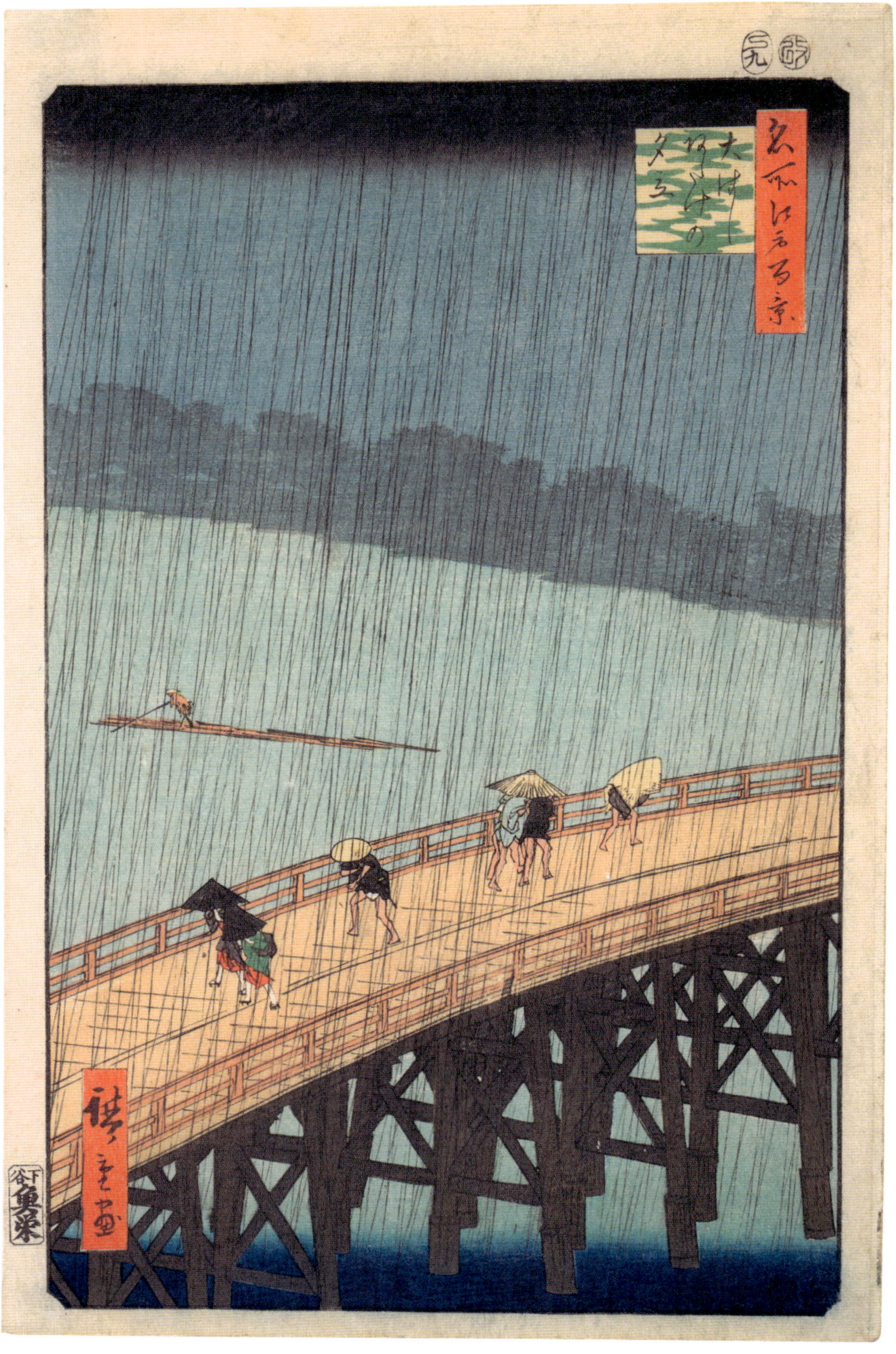
名所江戸百景
大はしあたけの夕立

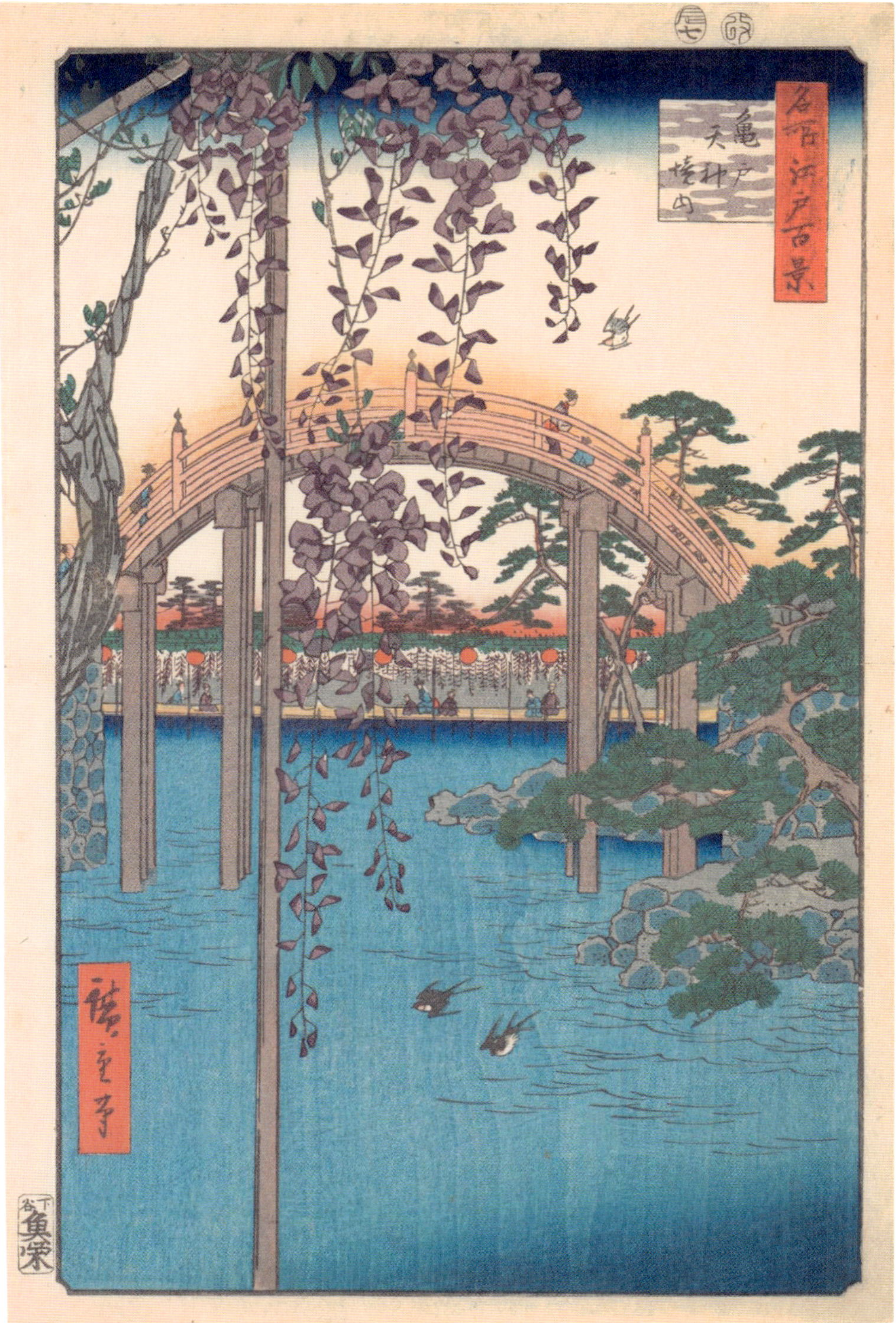
名所江戸百景
亀戸天神境内
廣重
下谷 魚栄

that Monet and his colleagues were originally known as *les Japonais*.[27]

Monet must have been exposed to Japanese art – given its ubiquity and popularity among his friends and contemporaries – well before he stepped into the fabled Zaandam grocery shop. Whatever the case, he bought up the grocer's entire supply of Japanese wrapping paper and then, over the decades that followed, began expanding his collection with the help of Parisian dealers and importers such as Tadamasa Hayashi, whose gallery in Paris became a hub for artists and collectors. Ultimately, more than 200 woodblock prints adorned the walls and stairwells of Monet's house in Giverny, including 23 by Hokusai and 48 by Hiroshige (figs 20 and 21).

The prints by these Japanese artists were known as *ukiyo-e*, which translates as 'pictures of the floating world'. The 'floating world' was a reference to the bustling entertainment districts of cities such as Edo (modern Tokyo) and Kyoto, with their theatres, restaurants, teahouses, brothels and kabuki performances – hence the reference to ephemeral pleasure-seeking. However, many artists also depicted more delicate rural scenes, beautifully composed landscapes with blossoming cherry orchards, boats navigating curvaceous streams, willow-draped lakes and delicate irises on the edges of ponds. Many included bridges, as in various prints from Hiroshige's masterpiece, *One Hundred Famous Views of Edo*, done in the 1850s.

Monet assimilated not only the subject matter of Japanese artists but also their practice of capturing motifs from various angles, across different seasons and under varied weather conditions. In the early 1830s Hokusai produced a series of landscape prints, *Thirty-Six Views of Mount Fuji*, in which each print – one of which was the iconic *The Great Wave off Kanagawa* – depicted Mount Fuji from a different perspective and in specific weather conditions sometimes referenced in the titles (*Storm below Mount Fuji* or *Beautiful Weather, Wind from the South*). An early enthusiast for Japanese prints, American painter John La Farge, summed up this practice in 1870, observing that Japanese prints 'are most charmingly sensitive to the colouring that makes up the appearance of different times of day, to the relations of colour which mark the different seasons so that their landscape efforts give us ... the illuminated air of the scene of action'.[28]

La Farge's comments perfectly anticipate Monet's approach to his series paintings – his groups of paintings of, for instance, grainstacks, Rouen Cathedral and poplars in the French countryside – in which he too tried to capture the ever-changing 'illuminated air' surrounding his motif. Furthermore, artists such as Hiroshige and Hokusai captured the beauty and essence of Japan by showcasing famous landscapes, historic landmarks and scenes of daily life that contributed to a sense of Japanese cultural pride and identity. Likewise, Monet's chosen scenes for his series paintings were redolent of an eternal and quintessential France. His subjects were not random but rather reflected a deep connection to France's landscape and heritage.[29] 'Monet's work above all expresses France', one art critic declared of Monet's series paintings, which revealed 'the beautiful elements of our countryside'[30] – a factor that no doubt contributed to their popular success in France.

Monet's intentions were not explicitly nationalist or patriotic, but his works undoubtedly tapped into a sense of national and cultural identity among the French people of his time. 'He has expressed everything that forms the soul of our race', declared one critic.[31] He criss-crossed France, painting landscapes and seascapes in various regions that offered distinctive geographical features and unique atmospheres: the rocky shores and seething waters of Belle-Île-en-Mer in Brittany; the rolling hills and winding river in the Creuse valley; the vibrant colours and intense sunlight of the Mediterranean; and the Normandy coast with its vast, windswept beaches unfurling beneath gloomy skies (fig. 22). Depicting scenes familiar to and beloved of French viewers, these canvases resonated with their shared

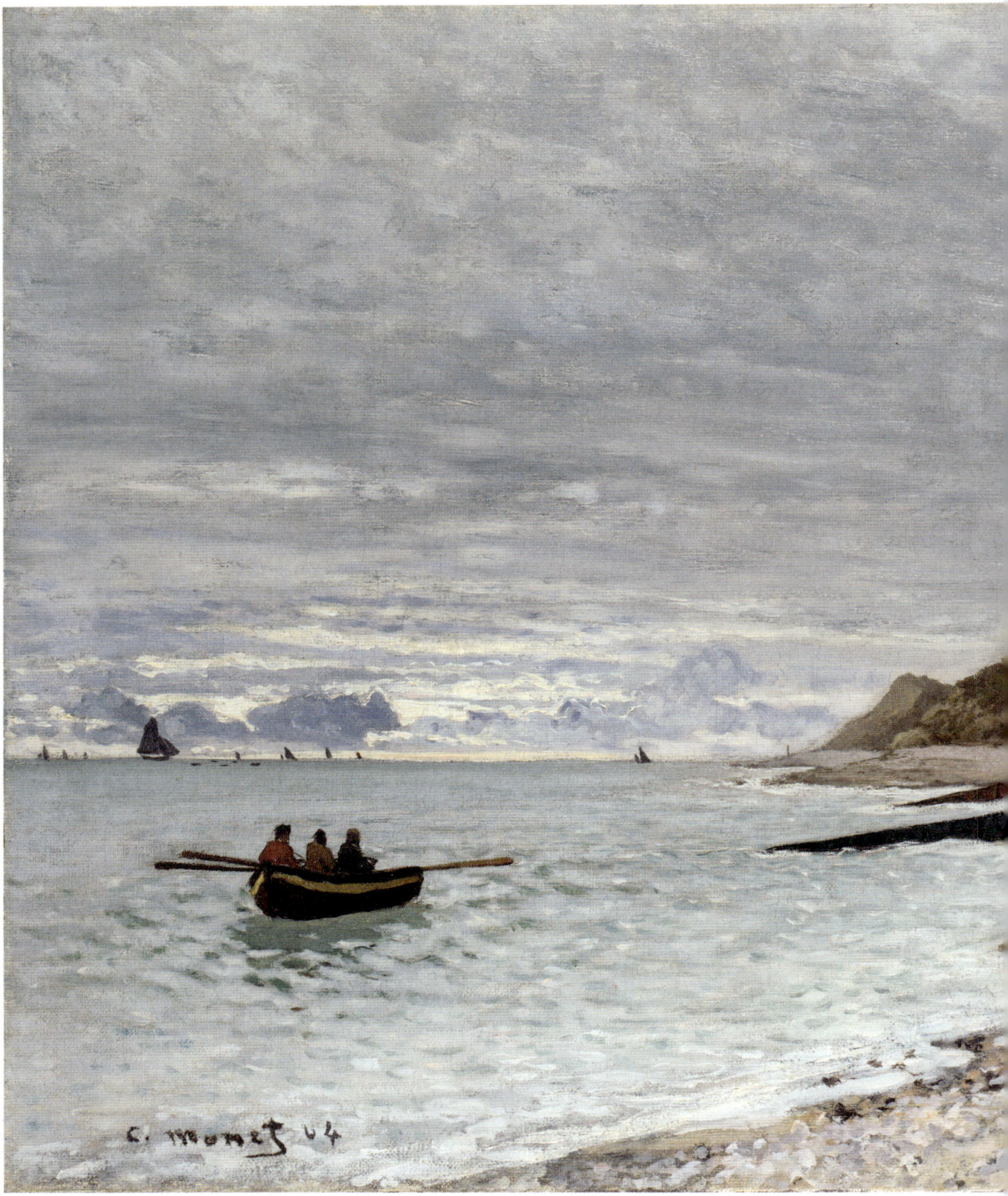
C. Monet 64

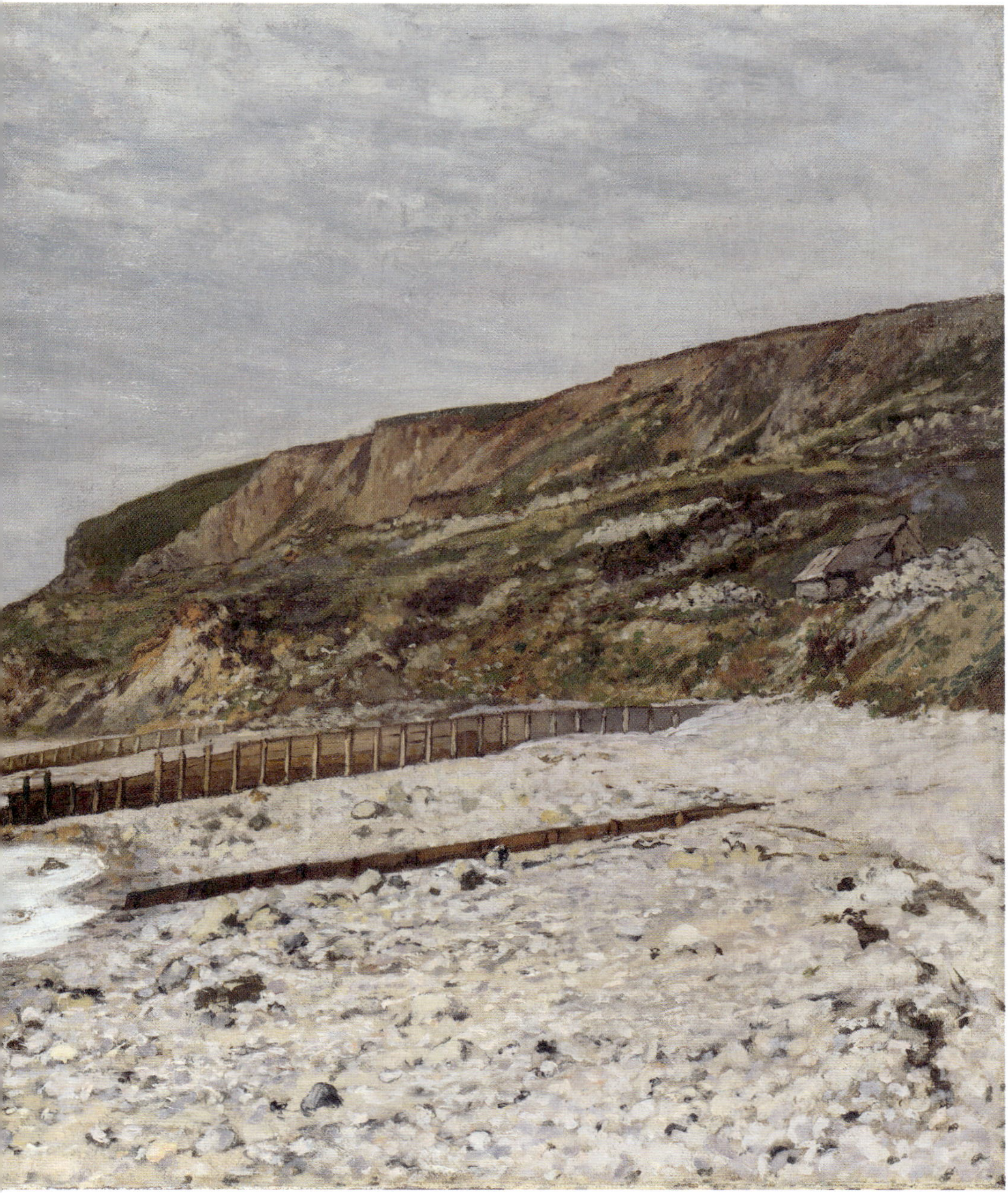

22 *La Pointe de la Hève, Sainte-Adresse*, 1864
Oil on canvas, 41 × 73 cm
The National Gallery, London

experiences of France's history and landscape, and they made him, as one critic wrote, 'our great national painter'.[32]

However, in the late 1890s the faith of Monet in his country – as well as the faith of many others – was to be comprehensively shattered, and his series of landscapes capturing the beauties of France would abruptly cease.

WE MUST CULTIVATE OUR GARDEN

One of the most notorious episodes in French history began unfolding in October 1894 when a Jewish officer in the French army, a captain from Alsace named Alfred Dreyfus, was arrested on a charge of treason, accused of passing military secrets to the German embassy in Paris. Although the evidence against Dreyfus was weak and circumstantial, a secret court-martial found him guilty (fig. 23). He was stripped of his rank and sentenced to life imprisonment on Devil's Island, a penal colony off French Guiana. The trial had serious irregularities, including suppressed evidence and secret testimony. In 1896, despite evidence pointing to a different culprit, the military refused to reopen the case. In 1897, Emile Zola began exposing the cover-up in *Le Figaro*, but when the newspaper found the story too incendiary he turned to his friend Georges Clemenceau, editor-in-chief of *L'Aurore* (fig. 24). In January 1898 his open letter 'J'Accuse ... !' charged the government with a miscarriage of justice and antisemitism. The letter split French society, with Dreyfus supporters seeing him as a victim of a corrupt government and military, while anti-Dreyfusards, including nationalists and Catholics, fiercely defended traditional values.

The Dreyfus Affair opened bitter rifts among the Impressionist painters. Degas and Renoir were vehement anti-Dreyfusards, the former (according to a witness) working himself into furious rages 'against the Jews' and the latter refusing to sign a petition in defence of Dreyfus, claiming he had joined the army only 'because the Jew likes to parade around in fancy uniforms'. Monet, on the other

23 Oswaldo Tofani (1849–1915)
'The Rennes case: Dreyfus before the War Council'
Engraving in *Le Petit Journal*, 20 August 1899

Le Petit Journal

Le Petit Journal
CHAQUE JOUR 5 CENTIMES
Le Supplément illustré
CHAQUE SEMAINE 5 CENTIMES

SUPPLÉMENT ILLUSTRÉ
Huit pages : CINQ centimes

ABONNEMENTS

	SIX MOIS	UN AN
SEINE ET SEINE-ET-OISE	2 fr.	3 fr. 50
DÉPARTEMENTS	2 fr.	4 fr.
ÉTRANGER	2 50	5 fr.

Dixième année — DIMANCHE 20 AOUT 1899 — Numéro 457

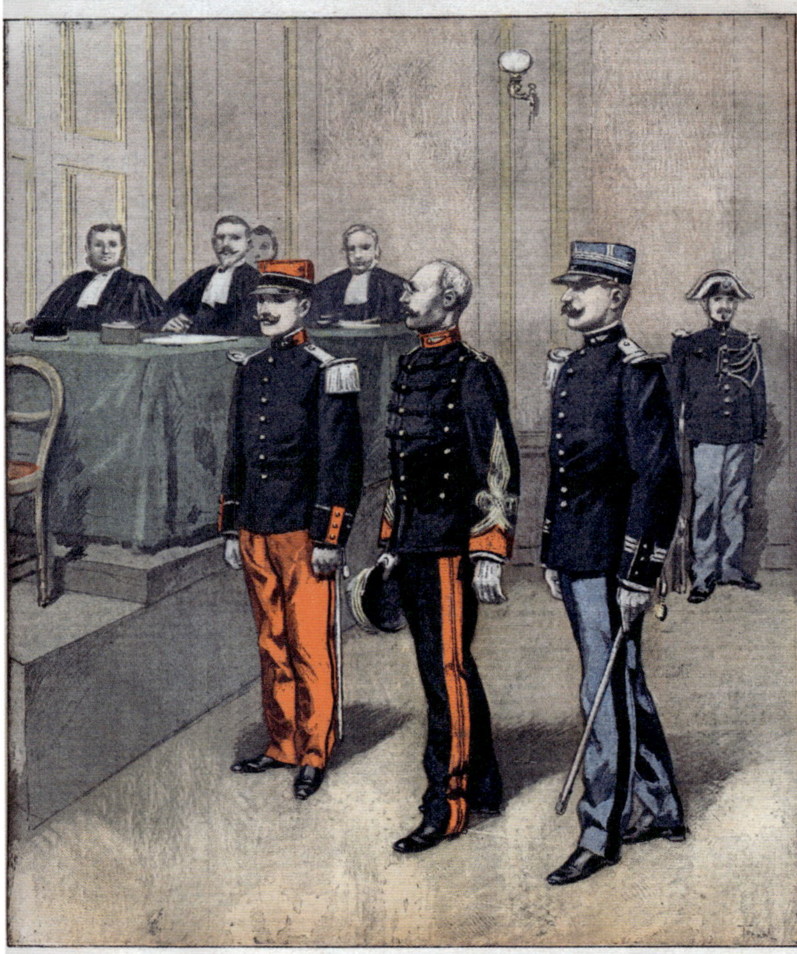

LE PROCÈS DE RENNES
Dreyfus amené au Conseil de guerre

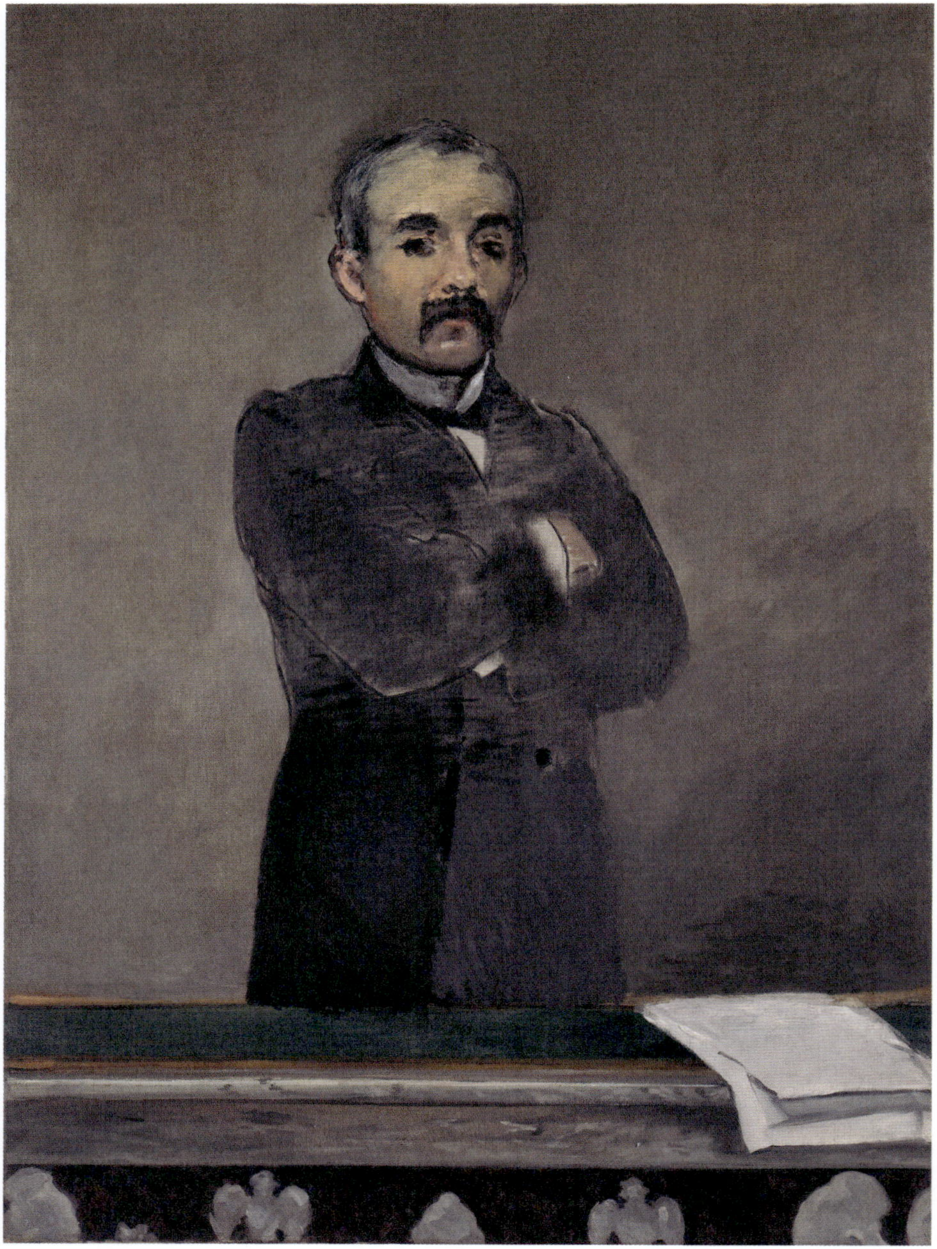

hand, signed the petition in *L'Aurore* and wrote three letters of support to Zola. 'I want to tell you', read one of them, 'how much I admire your courageous and heroic conduct.' He also made a gift of one of his paintings to Clemenceau – a friend since the 1860s – for his part in the 'fine campaign on behalf of right and truth'.[33]

Monet's friendship with Clemenceau and his admiration for Zola – a former habitué of the Café Guerbois and an early supporter in print of the Impressionists – meant he became intimately and unavoidably aware of unsavoury forces at work in French society. One art historian has persuasively argued that Monet abandoned his French-themed series paintings because the Dreyfus Affair had altered his vision of France.[34] To be sure, Monet had begun painting his water-lily pond before Zola published 'J'Accuse ... !', and before the sinister depths of French nationalism and antisemitism became evident. However, from the late 1890s until his death in 1926 Monet was to paint more than 500 canvases, only a dozen of which have recognisably French subject matter. Instead, the vast majority, literally hundreds of paintings, would depict a world of his own creation, more private and intimate – and more foreign in appearance – than his cathedrals and grainstacks. Rather like the hero of Voltaire's novel *Candide* (1759), he decided the best course of action was to cultivate his garden.

After completing more than 60 canvases in 1897, including two dozen of his *Mornings on the Seine* series, Monet barely touched his palette and brushes in 1898. This uncharacteristic hiatus was caused not merely by the Dreyfus Affair but, even more, by the illness, followed by the death from cancer in February 1899, of his 32-year-old stepdaughter Suzanne. She was the daughter of his second wife, Alice Hoschedé, with whom he lived following the death in 1879, also from cancer, of his first wife Camille. Monet had therefore found himself raising two sons of his own, Jean and Michel, as well as Alice's four girls and two boys from a previous marriage (fig. 25). This blended family

24 Edouard Manet (1832–1883)
Portrait of Georges Clemenceau, 1879–80
Oil on canvas, 115.9 × 88.2 cm
Kimbell Art Museum, Fort Worth, Texas

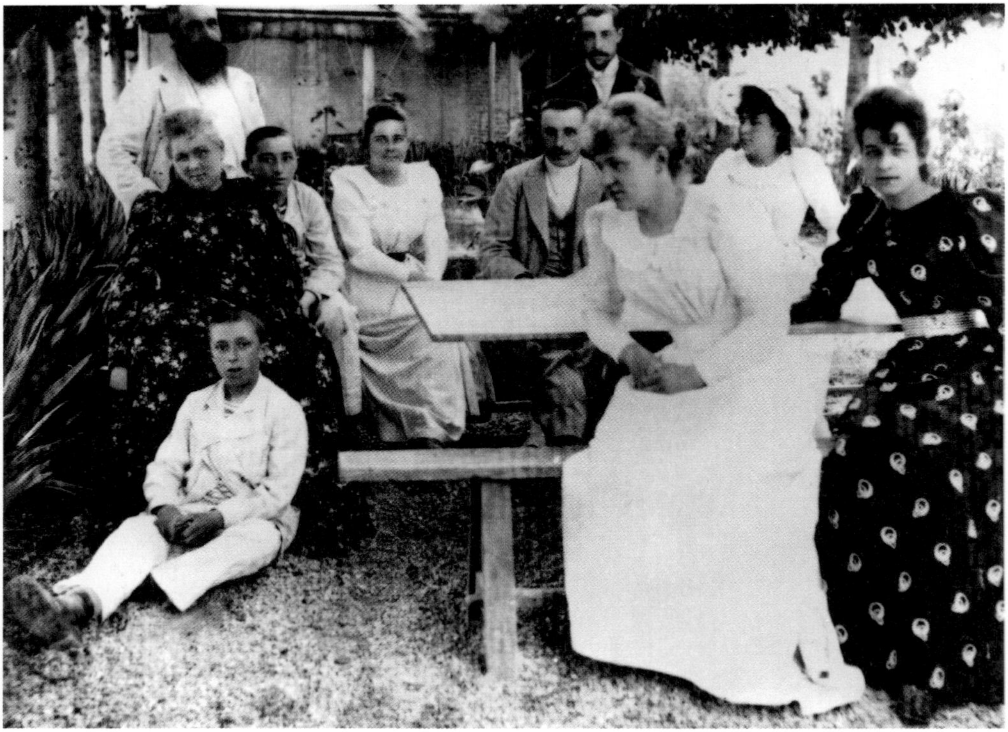

was given an extra stir in 1897 when Jean Monet married Alice's daughter Blanche. Five years before that, Suzanne, one of Monet's favourite models, had married Theodore Butler, a young American painter. Butler was part of an American colony at Giverny, young artists drawn to the area by its unique atmospheric effects and the fame of its resident artist. Monet had been very much opposed to the match: 'To marry a painter,' he complained to Alice: 'how annoying.'[35] An earlier suitor, another member of the American colony named John Leslie Breck, had unceremoniously been sent packing following attempts to woo Blanche. However, in Butler's case the outraged paterfamilias was eventually mollified by the young man's bona fides as the son of a prosperous line of bankers.

25 The Monet and Hoschedé families at Giverny, 1880s
Musée Marmottan Monet, Paris

Alice was left devastated and inconsolable after Suzanne's death, visiting her grave in the nearby churchyard each morning. Meanwhile, Monet's long spell of inactivity persisted over the following months as he and Alice grieved and tried to cope. However, in the summer of 1899 he took up his brushes and paintbox, crossed the road and railway at the bottom of his garden and – as he was to do thousands of times in the decades to follow – sat down by the edge of his water-lily pond, ready to paint.

Over the course of the next two dozen years, Monet would produce hundreds of paintings of his water lilies (fig. 26). He entrenched himself beside the pond with such unwavering determination that whenever he needed a haircut the village barber was summoned to perform his duties while the master sat before his easel. 'You have launched a rocket at infinity', Clemenceau was later to write of Monet's enduring obsession and staggeringly ambitious project – what he called his *grande décoration*.[36] In 1927, the year following Monet's death, 22 of these paintings were unveiled in what was officially known as the Musée Claude-Monet à l'Orangerie des Tuileries – almost 90 metres of canvas showing his pond at various times of the day, from pinkish sunrise to sulphurous sunset. The Orangerie would eventually become known as the 'Sistine Chapel of Impressionism'.[37]

However, the public first got a glimpse of Monet's visions of his water-lily pond and its Japanese bridge almost three decades earlier. On 22 November 1900, an exhibition of his work opened at the Galerie Durand-Ruel in rue Laffitte, the scene, over the previous decade, of so many of his triumphant exhibitions. Monet made a rare trip to Paris for the occasion, his eyes twinkling and one hand 'foraging in the silky waves of his long beard where a few blond threads still mingle with the snowy white'.[38] Dedicated to what a newspaper called 'the latest colour sensations of Claude Monet', the show featured some 30 of his works, including canvases of the Normandy coast and the Creuse valley.[39] Critics and collectors would have

26 *Water-Lilies, Setting Sun*, about 1907
Oil on canvas, 73 × 92.7 cm
The National Gallery, London

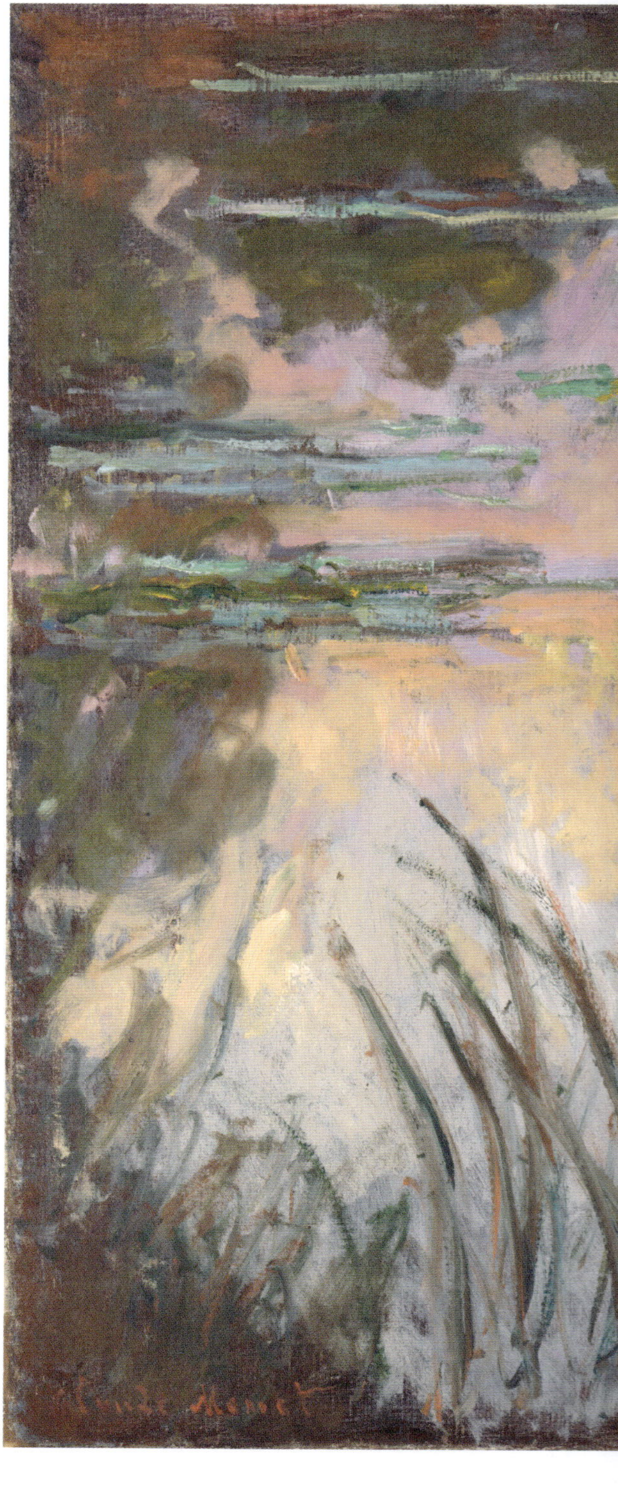

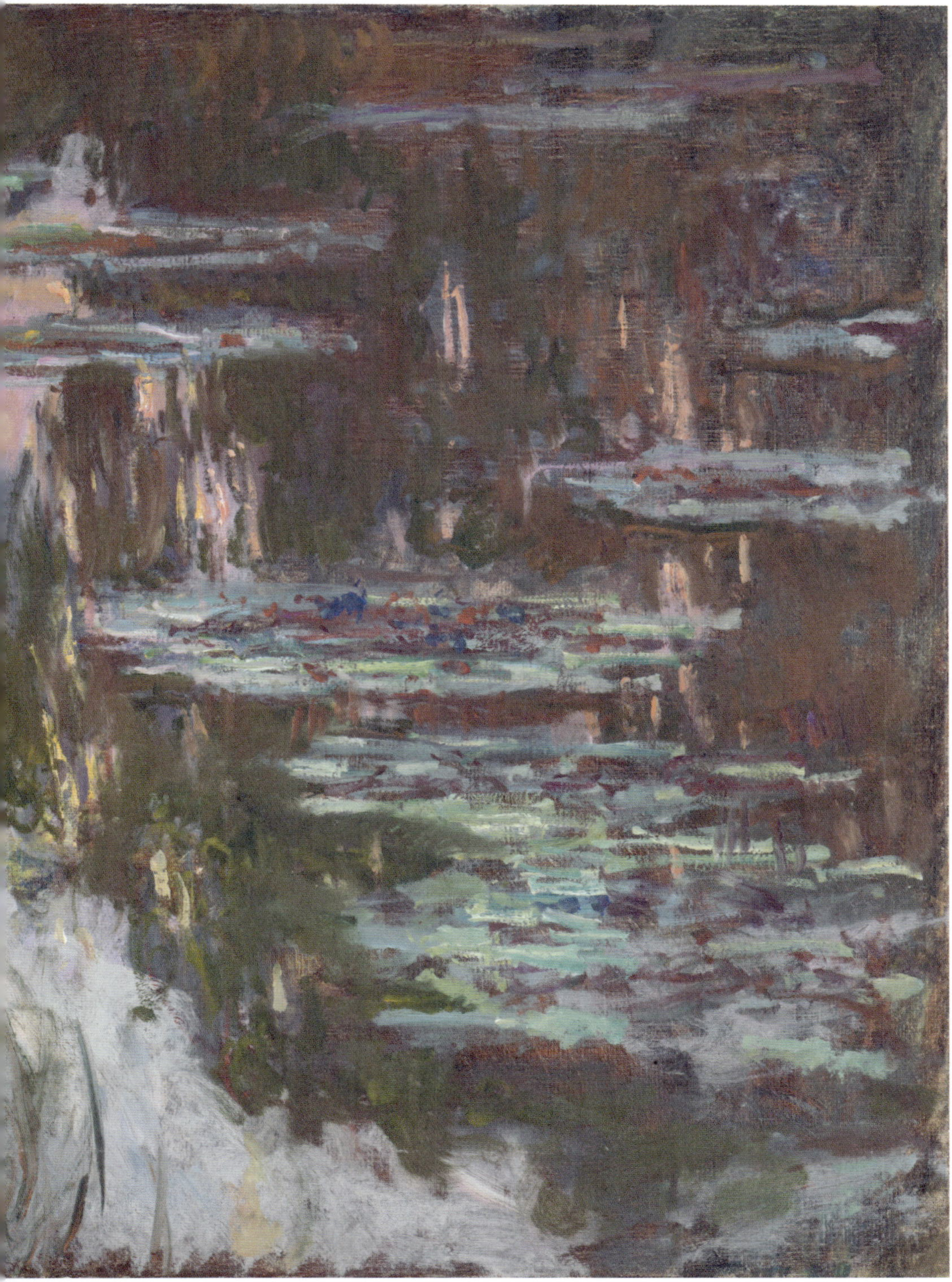

seen examples of many of these paintings, but a dozen others – those depicting his Japanese bridge arching above the pond – were entirely new. The reviews were as rapturous as the exhibition was commercially successful, with Louisine Havemeyer, for example, purchasing not one but two paintings of the Japanese bridge. The National Gallery's canvas, *The Water-Lily Pond*, was sold even before it went on display with Durand-Ruel: one of Monet's other dealers, the Galerie Bernheim-Jeune, bought it from him in 1899 and then sold it to the banker Georges Kohn. Already the owner of several other Monet paintings, Kohn was an example of the affluent and discerning Parisian clients who, for the previous decade, had been buying his work.

It can have come as no great surprise that Monet took a bridge as the subject of his latest series of paintings. Bridges had been a favoured subject of the Impressionists, no doubt inspired in part by the many bridges appearing in the works of Hiroshige and Hokusai. Gustave Caillebotte depicted the Pont de l'Europe, Renoir the bridge at Chatou, and Sisley the bridges at Moret-sur-Loing and Villeneuve-la-Garenne. Pissarro captured the Pont Boieldieu over the Seine at Rouen, as well as, on trips to London, Old Chelsea Bridge and Charing Cross Bridge. In the mid-1870s, Monet produced a number of canvases featuring both the road and railway bridges spanning the Seine at Argenteuil, including *The Argenteuil Bridge* and *The Wooden Bridge* (fig. 27). He even acquired a small studio boat that allowed him to float along the Seine and paint the bridges from various angles and distances.

Painting bridges over stretches of water presented an artist with interesting structural forms, geometric shapes and spatial relationships, adding depth, perspective and visual interest – including reflections – to a scene. If earlier landscapists such as Camille Corot had depicted medieval stone bridges, the Impressionists typically chose instead to paint modern structures, emphasising their

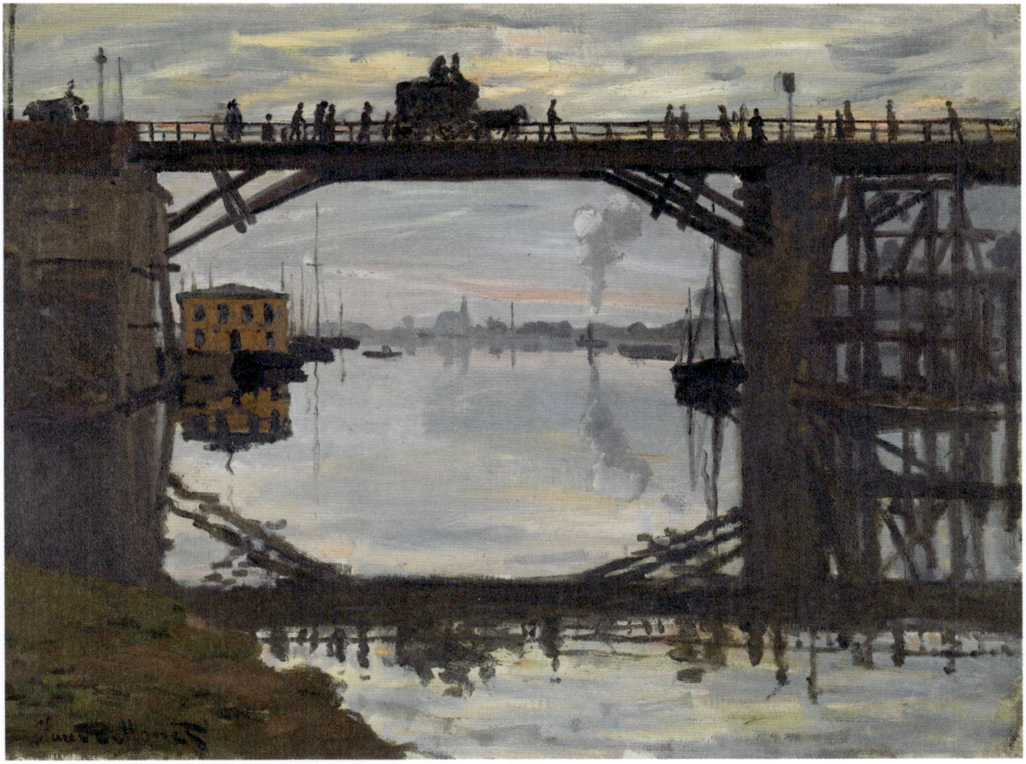

27 *The Wooden Bridge*, 1872
Oil on canvas, 54 × 73 cm
Private collection, on loan to the National Gallery of Canada, Ottawa

girders and iron trellises, often with oblique perspectives and steam from locomotives or billows of industrial smoke. Monet's paintings of the Argenteuil bridges, as well as his depiction of the Pont de l'Europe – featuring a sharply angled view and plumes of sooty smoke – vividly captured the bustling energy of the modern urban world of traffic, crowds and industry. One of his most striking bridge paintings was *Men unloading Coal*, where he depicted the road bridge at Asnières vaulting over an industrial scene of labourers unloading coal from barges moored in the Seine (fig. 28). Smokestacks fume in the distance while another bridge, located at Clichy, is faintly visible through the murky haze.

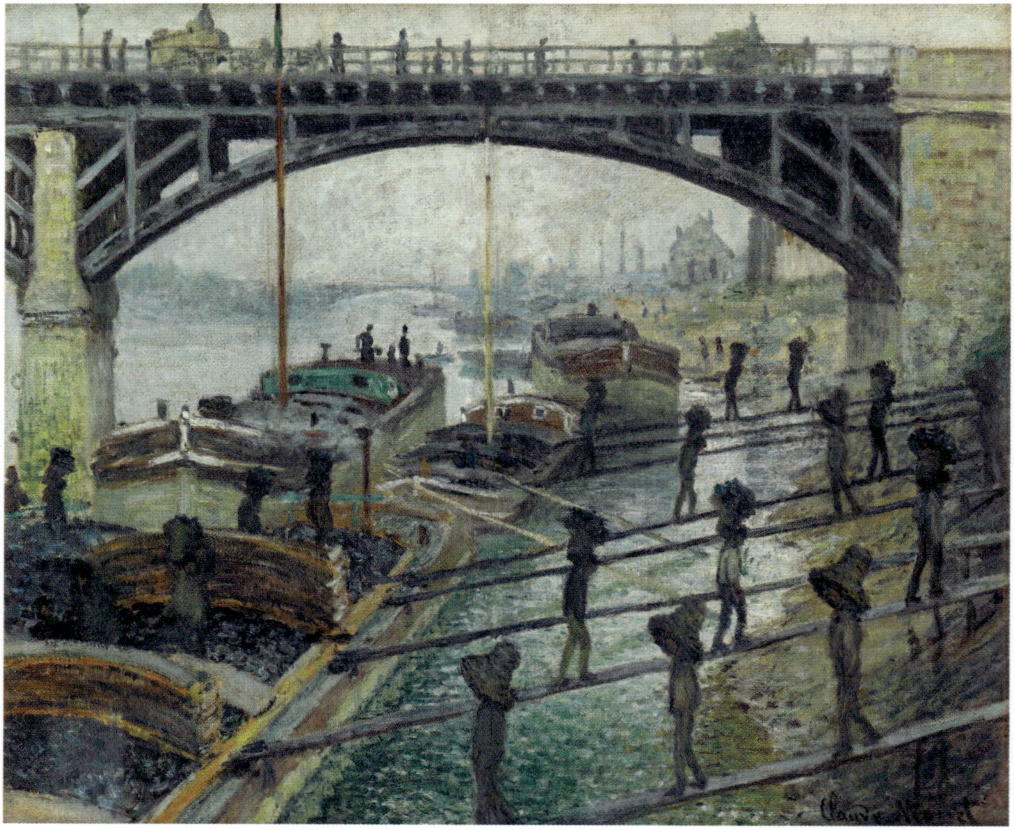

In Monet's paintings of his pond, the Japanese bridge likewise arches horizontally across the picture plane, its gentle curve dividing the canvas into two distinct sections. Unlike his earlier works, however, these compositions lack crowds, industry and a distinct sense of place, except perhaps for a subtle nod to Japan. They offer, by contrast, a more intimate and timeless experience, portraying tranquil scenes of lush vegetation, calm waters and soothing colour harmonies. As in all his series paintings, Monet skilfully captures the scene at different times of the day, transforming the bridge, willows and water lilies, as the sunlight and

28 *Men unloading Coal,* about 1875
Oil on canvas,
54 × 65.5 cm
Musée d'Orsay, Paris

shadows change, from greens and blues to pinks, reds, mauves and purples (fig. 29). The bustle and movement take place not within the canvases themselves, as in the earlier bridge paintings, but from canvas to canvas as he endeavours to capture and freeze each passing moment, each flicker of light or shift of shadow.

The canvas in the National Gallery (see fig. 1) was purchased in 1927 for the Tate Gallery in London with funds provided by Samuel Courtauld, the world's largest manufacturer of rayon and – thanks to his wealth and discriminating tastes – one of Britain's greatest patrons of the arts. *The Water-Lily Pond* was transferred from the Tate to the National Gallery in 1961, one of the Gallery's 14 canvases by the master (fig. 30 is another). It shows a slightly different perspective from a number of the other versions, with the bridge raised higher and the water lilies displayed more prominently in the foreground. The scene beautifully encapsulates both continuity and transition. This bridge with no beginning and no end symbolises the fluid passage from one state into another, spanning not only physical spaces but also emotional and temporal realms. Painted at the twilight of the nineteenth century, the bridge is poised between the waning of one age and the dawn of another. This temporal liminality mirrors Monet's personal transition. Having lost his beloved Suzanne, he channelled his grief into his work, seeking solace by contemplating and capturing the beauty of his garden – a lifelong dialogue with nature's fleeting moments and eternal rhythms. The Japanese bridge became a gateway leading him on a serene yet poignant journey, and in its endless arc we find a reflection of our own transitions, eternally bridging the old and the new, the past and the present, the sorrowful and the sublime.

29 *Water-Lily Basin, Pink Harmony*, 1900
Oil on canvas, 90 × 100 cm
Musée d'Orsay, Paris

Overleaf:
30 *The Thames below Westminster*, about 1871
Oil on canvas, 47 × 73 cm
The National Gallery, London

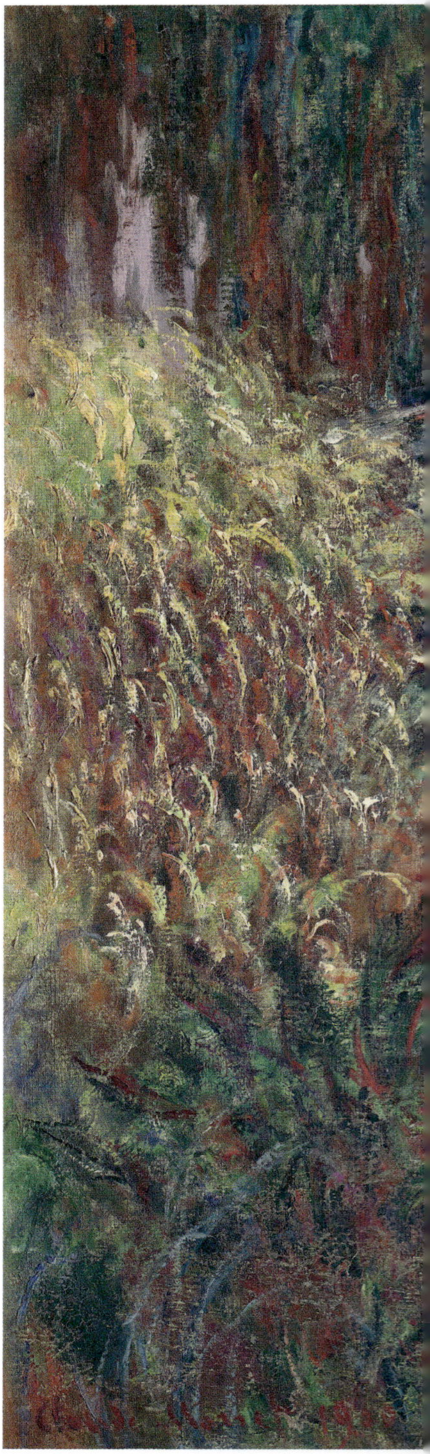

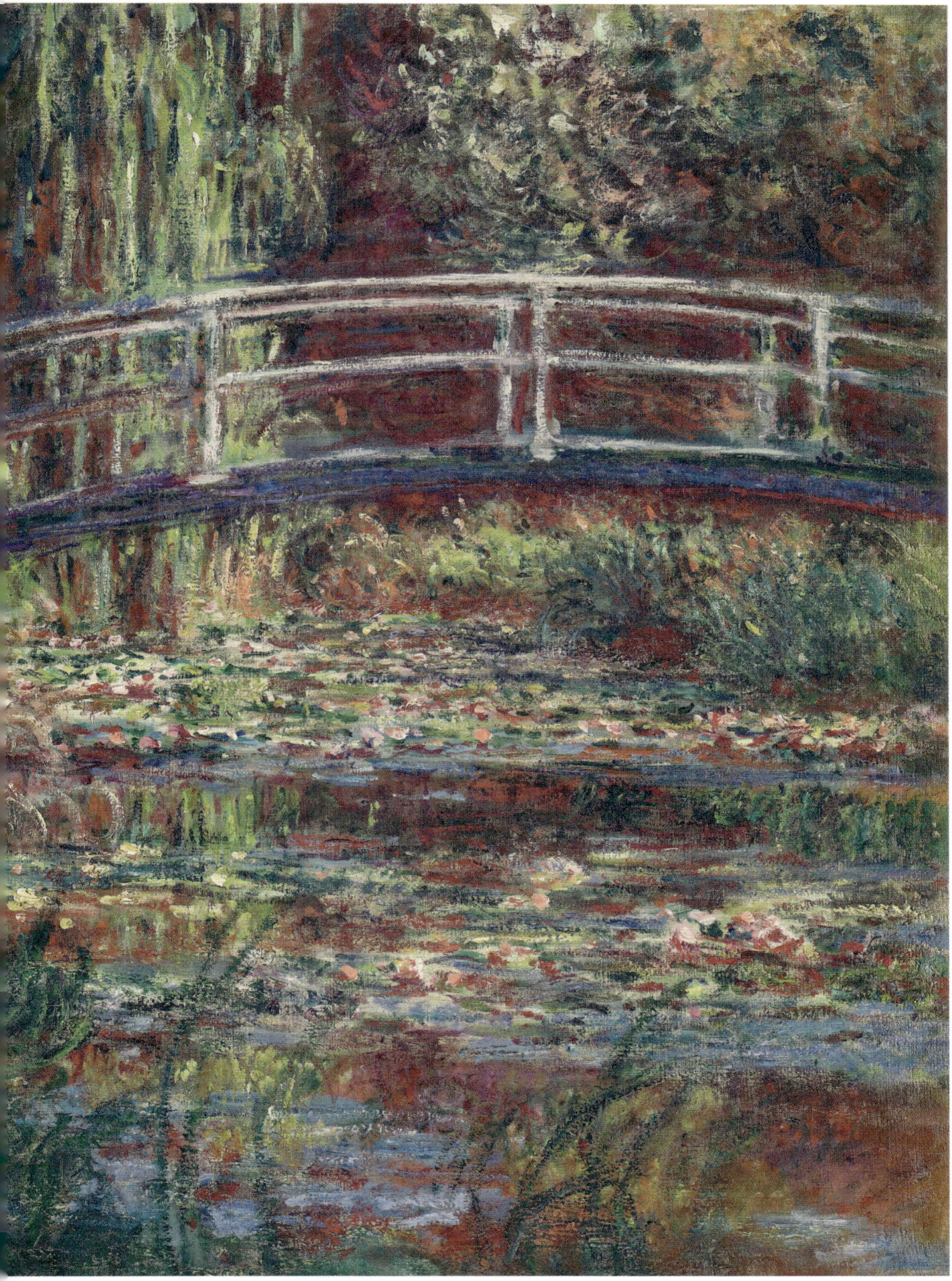

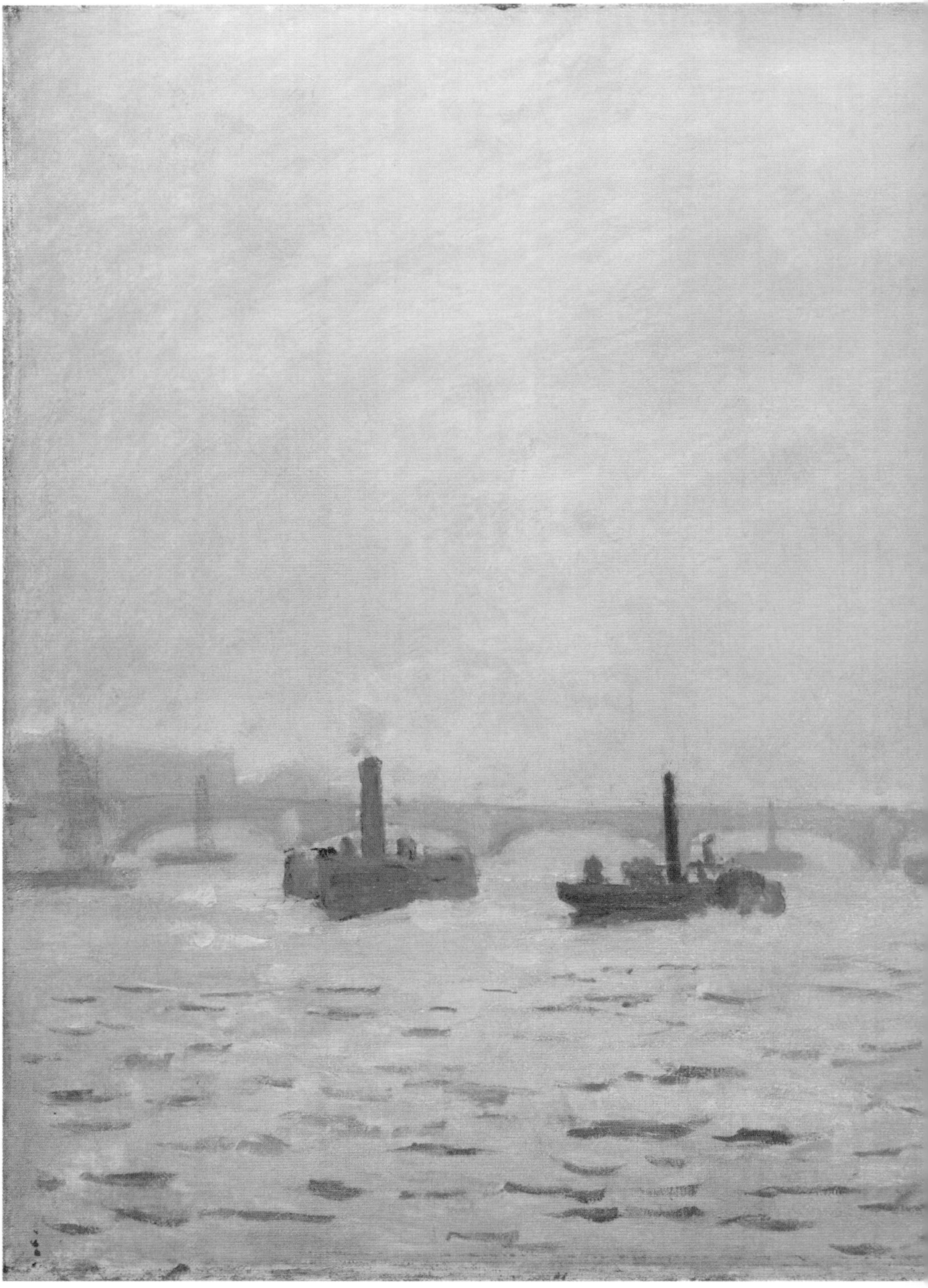

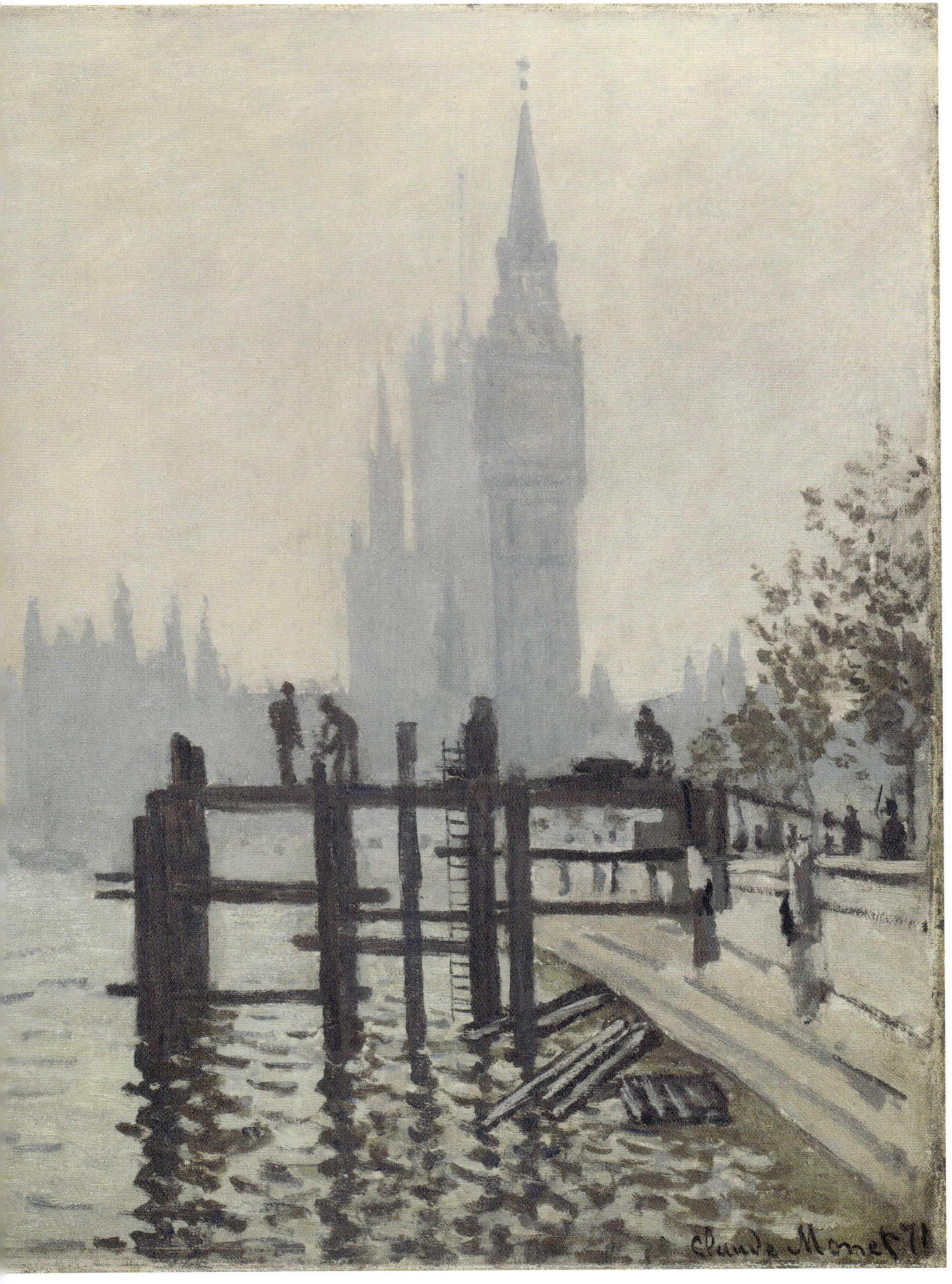
Claude Monet 71

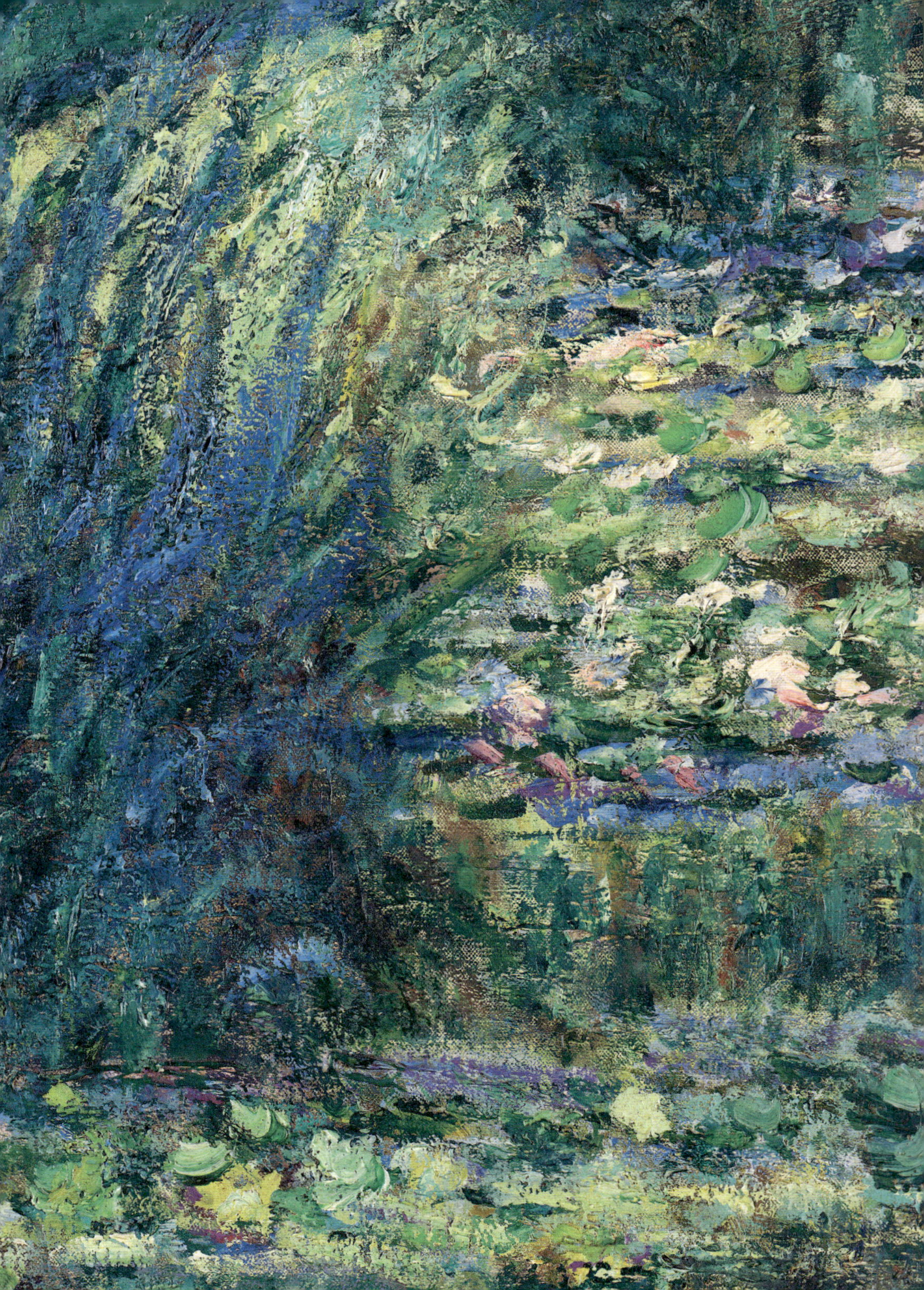

NOTES

1 All information on this 1897 visit to Giverny is taken from M. Guillemot, 'Claude Monet', *La Revue illustrée*, 15 December 1897 (unpaginated); the author's translations.
2 G. Geffroy, 'Exposition Claude Monet', *Le Gaulois*, 16 June 1898, p. 2.
3 Gimpel 1966, p. 8.
4 All quotations are from Guillemot, 'Claude Monet', 1897.
5 A. Arnyvelde, 'Chez le peintre de la lumière', *Je Sais Tout*, 15 January 1914, p. 30.
6 F. Thiébault-Sisson, 'Claude Monet, les années d'épreuve', *Le Temps*, 26 November 1900, p. 3.
7 Ibid.
8 Quoted in Wildenstein 1996, p. 12.
9 Thiébault-Sisson, 'Claude Monet, les années d'épreuve', 1900, p. 3.
10 Ibid.
11 Ibid.
12 Ibid.
13 Guillemot, 'Claude Monet', 1897.
14 Wildenstein 1974–91, vol. 1, letter 50.
15 L. Leroy, 'Exhibition des Impressionnistes', *Le Charivari*, 25 April 1874, pp. 319–20.
16 *New York Tribune*, 26 April 1886, p. 3.
17 Weitzenhoffer 1984, p. 74.
18 Bourguignon 2007, p. 22.
19 Levine 1994, p. 215.
20 G. Clemenceau, 'La Révolution des Cathédrales', *La Justice*, 20 May 1895, p. 1.
21 M. Moser, 'Rapport du M. Moser', in *Rapports du Jury International*, Paris 1889, p. 13.
22 Wildenstein 1974–91, vol. 5, letter 2319.
23 Quoted in Tucker 1989, p. 270.
24 C. Pelletan in *Les Merveilles de l'Exposition de 1878*, Paris 1878, pp. 226, 231.
25 J. Conder, *Landscape Gardening in Japan*, Tokyo 1893, p. 90.
26 G. Truffaut, 'Le Jardin de Claude Monet', *Jardinage*, November 1924.
27 J. Castagnary, 'Les Impressionnistes', *Le Siècle*, 29 April 1874, p. 3.
28 Quoted in Bromfield 1977, p. 380.
29 For this argument, see Tucker 1989, p. 251.
30 R. Bouyer, quoted in ibid., p. 275.
31 Bouyer quoted in ibid.
32 Ibid.
33 For all of these responses, see Nord 2000, pp. 102–4.
34 See Tucker 1989, p. 256.
35 Wildenstein 1974–91, letter 1151.
36 Clemenceau 1928, p. 19.
37 Masson 2008, p. 191.
38 Thiébault-Sisson, 'Claude Monet, les années d'épreuve', 1900, p. 3.
39 'L'impressionnisme: Exposition d'oeuvres nouvelles de Claude Monet', *La Justice*, 5 December 1900, p. 1.

FURTHER READING

Bourguignon 2007
K.M. Bourguignon (ed.), *Impressionist Giverny: A Colony of Artists, 1885–1915*, Giverny 2007

Bromfield 1977
D.J. Bromfield, 'The Art of Japan in Later Nineteenth Century Europe: Problems of Art Criticism and Theory', PhD dissertation, University of Leeds 1977

Clemenceau 1928
G. Clemenceau, *Claude Monet: Les Nymphéas*, Paris 1928

Gimpel 1966
R. Gimpel, *Diary of an Art Dealer*, trans. J. Rosenberg, New York 1966

King 2017
R. King, *Mad Enchantment: Claude Monet and the Painting of the Water Lilies*, London 2017

Levine 1994
S.Z. Levine, *Monet, Narcissus, and Self-Reflection: The Modernist Myth of the Self*, Chicago 1994

Masson 2008
A. Masson, 'Monet the Founder' [1952], trans. T. Maloon, in G.T.M. Shackleford et al. (eds), *Monet and the Impressionists*, Sydney 2008

Nord 2000
P. Nord, *Impressionists and Politics: Art and Democracy in the Nineteenth Century*, London and New York 2000

Tucker 1989
P.H. Tucker, *Monet in the '90s: The Series Paintings*, New Haven, CT 1989

Weitzenhoffer 1984
F. Weitzenhoffer, 'The Earliest American Collectors of Monet', in J. Rewald and F. Weitzenhoffer (eds), *Aspects of Monet: A Symposium on the Artist's Life and Times*, New York 1984

Wildenstein 1974–91
D. Wildenstein, *Claude Monet: Biographie et catalogue raisonné*, 5 vols, Lausanne and Paris 1974–91

Wildenstein 1996
D. Wildenstein, *Monet, or the Triumph of Impressionism*, Cologne and Paris 1996

PICTURE CREDITS

© The National Gallery, London: figs 1, 6, 8, 9, 11, 12, 22, 26, 30.

© Archives of American Art, Smithsonian Institution, Washington, DC: figs 2, 5, 19.

The Metropolitan Museum of Art, New York © The Metropolitan Museum of Art/Art Resource/Scala, Florence: fig. 3; © The Metropolitan Museum of Art, New York: figs 20, 21.

Musée Marmottan Monet, Paris © musée Marmottan Monet/Studio Christian Baraja SLB: figs 4, 14; © musée Marmottan Monet: figs 10, 17, 25.

© The Art Institute of Chicago: figs 7, 16.

Musée d'Orsay, Paris © GrandPalaisRmn (musée d'Orsay)/Benoît Touchard: fig. 13; © Musée d'Orsay, Dist. GrandPalaisRmn/Patrice Schmidt: fig. 28; © GrandPalaisRmn (musée d'Orsay)/Adrien Didierjean: fig. 29.

© National Galleries of Scotland, Edinburgh: fig. 15.

© Roger Viollet/Getty Images: fig. 18.

© Stefano Bianchetti/Bridgeman Images: fig. 23.

Kimbell Art Museum, Fort Worth, Texas © Vidimages/Alamy Stock Photo: fig. 24.

Private Collection, on loan to the National Gallery of Canada, Ottawa © Vidimages/Alamy Stock Photo: fig. 27.

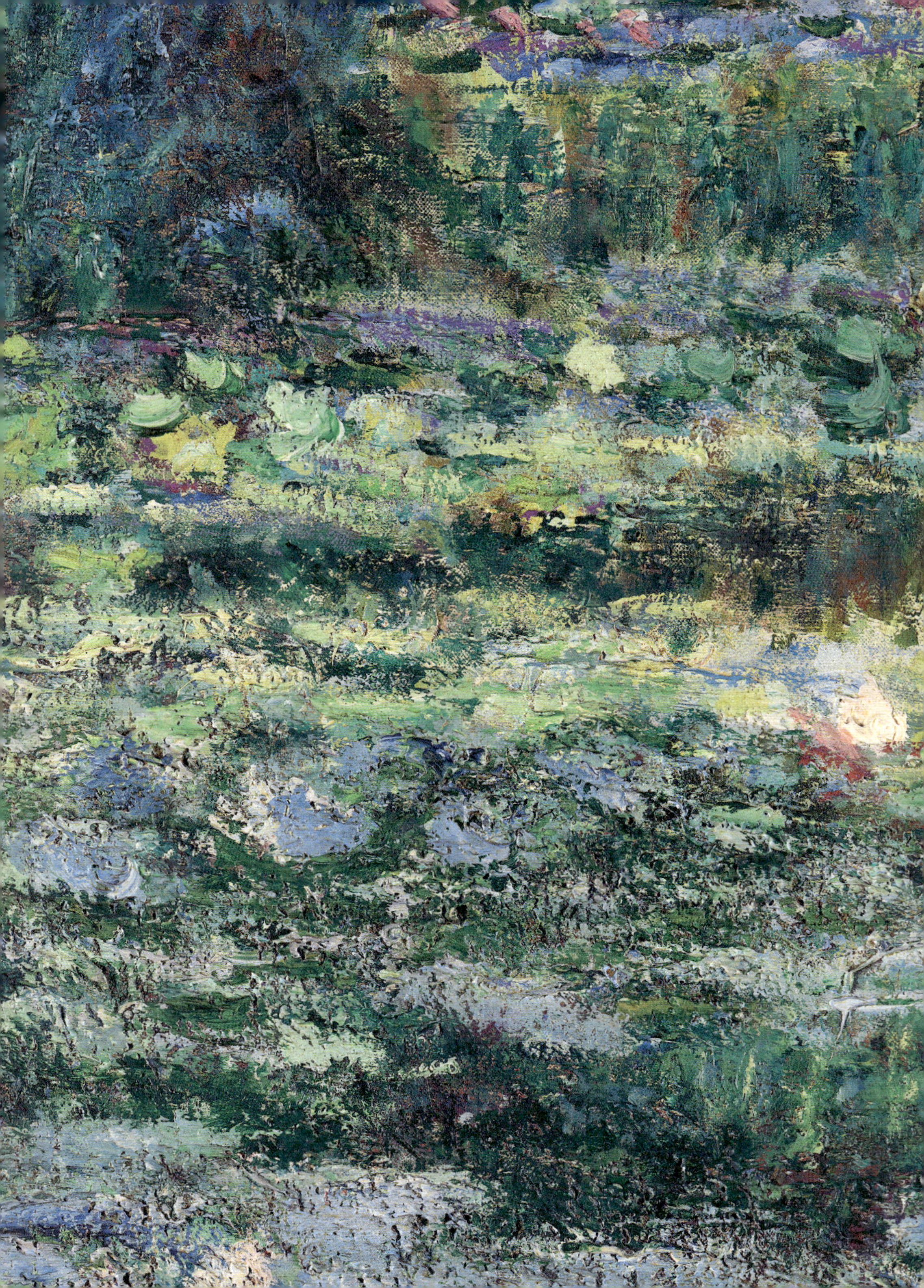

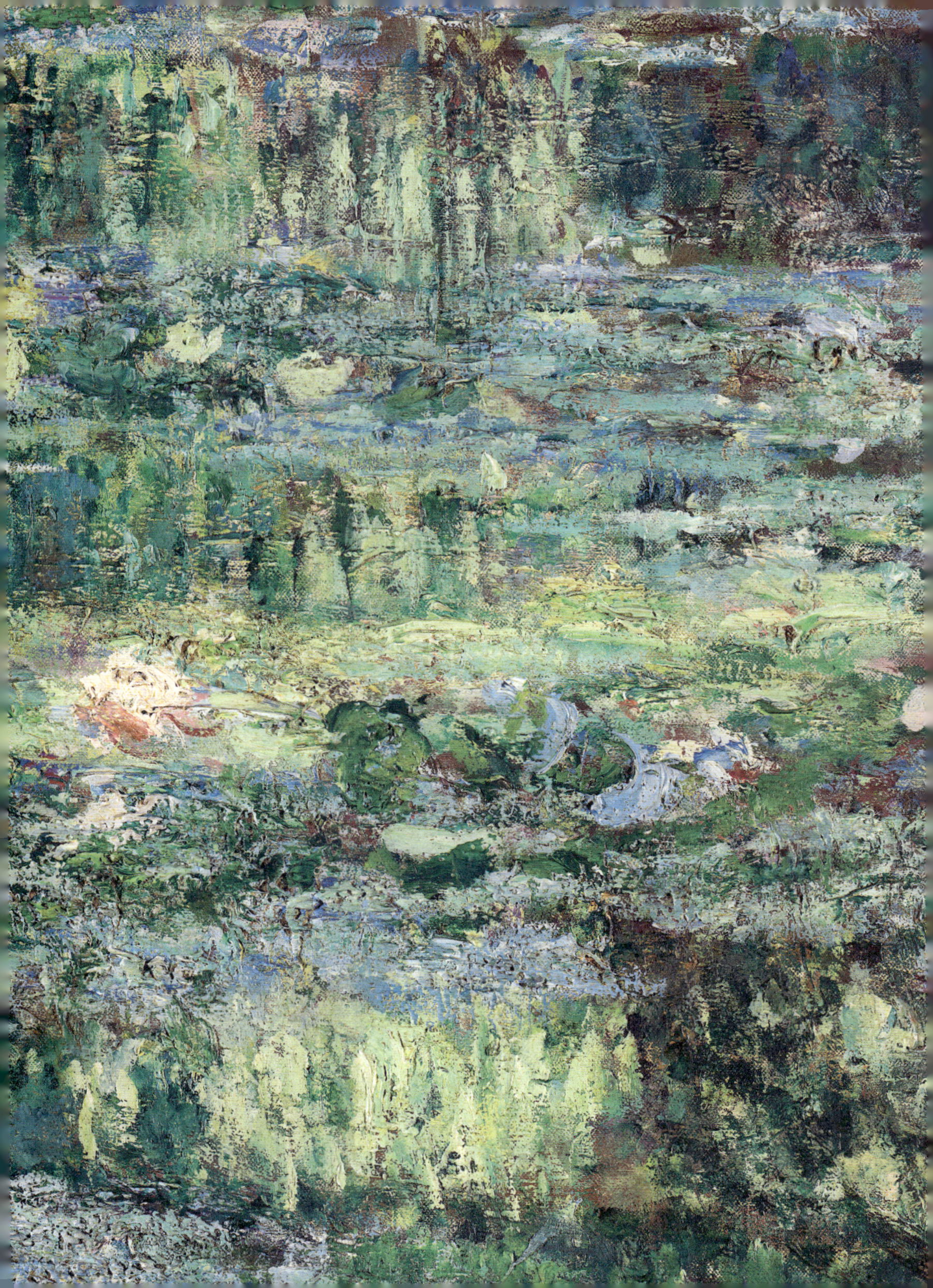

NG**200**

200 YEARS OF THE NATIONAL GALLERY

Ross King is the author of numerous books on French and Italian art and history, including *Claude Monet and the Painting of The Water Lilies*.

© National Gallery Global Limited 2025

The author has asserted his rights under the Copyright, Designs and Patents Act, 1988, to be identified as the Author of this work.

All rights reserved. No part of this publication may be transmitted in any form or by any means, electronic or mechanical, including photocopy, recording, or any storage and retrieval system, without the prior permission in writing from the publisher.

Authorised Representative in the EU Details: Easy Access System Europe, Mustamäe tee 50, 10621 Tallinn, Estonia, gpsr.requests@easproject.com

First published in 2025 by
National Gallery Global Limited
Trafalgar Square
London WC2N 5DN
www.shop.nationalgallery.org.uk

ISBN: 978 1 85709 733 7
1054457

British Library Cataloguing-in-Publication Data
A catalogue record is available from the British Library

Publisher: Laura Lappin
Senior Project Editor: Catherine Hooper
Copy-editor: Robert Davies
Proofreader: Caroline Ellerby
Picture Researcher: Rebecca Thornton
Production: Davina Cheung

Designed by Sandra Zellmer, with Katrin Zellmer
Origination by DL Imaging, London
Printed in Italy by Printer Trento

All works are by Claude Monet (1840–1926) unless otherwise stated.

All measurements give height before width.

Cover and pp. 4, 58, 62–3: details from Claude Monet, *The Water-Lily Pond*, 1899 (fig. 1)

MIX
Paper | Supporting responsible forestry
FSC® C015829
FSC www.fsc.org